CALLING IT OFF

Memoir of an *Almost* Bride

KATHERINE ROSE WOLLER

**LANDON
HAIL**
PRESS

The author gratefully acknowledges permission to reprint the following:

"Home": Words and Music by Jade Castrinos and Alex Ebert
Copyright © 2009 Jadey Rae, BMG Monarch and Caravan Touchdown
All Rights for Jadey Rae Administered by Songs of Kobalt Music Publishing
All Rights for BMG Monarch and Caravan Touchdown Administered by BMG Rights Management (US) LLC
All Rights Reserved Used by Permission
Reprinted by Permission of Hal Leonard LLC

Paperback ISBN: 978-1-959955-57-3
Hardback ISBN: 978-1-959955-58-0

Cover design by Rich Johnson, Spectacle Photo
Photo by Angelli Nguyen
Creative direction by Samantha Joy
Published by Landon Hail Press

To my daughter, Rose Darling.
May you have the strength to love without abandon,
the courage to walk away from that which does not
serve you, and the conviction to trust yourself,
always and forever.

Contents

Disclaimer

In the interest of full disclosure, I want to point out that this book is my subjective retelling and my best possible memory of the events, conversations, and emotions surrounding my engagement, failed wedding, and post-fallout recovery as they happened to *me*. I scoured old photos, Google planning documents, spreadsheets, and text messages–you name it, I reviewed it–to reconstruct what happened, and even so, this is an admittedly imperfect reconstruction. There's no doubt I've bungled some of the timeline, details, and conversations, but this is truly my best attempt. To those of you who lived this with me, you all have every right to remember it differently.

But this is *my* story.

As such, I endeavored to include only the bits central to my experience and did not intend to include anything hurtful or disparaging to anyone else. I changed names, removed nonessential, distinguishing characteristics to obscure identities, and generalized where needed to protect the privacy of those involved. I knowingly omitted details and/or specifics that might be damning or painful or downright hurtful to others.

I tell my story with love and respect for each and every person who played a part, no matter how big or small.

Author's Note

To the reader,

I know you want to get to the juicy stuff, but **before** we jump into our journey together, I need to take a moment to address a few aspects of my story. Mainly, I am well aware it's absurd.

If you have been lucky enough to experience an engagement or wedding season of your own, then you are probably aware it tends to be an over-the-top and even out-of-character season of life. Even if you have not chosen this path, one of your girlfriends has probably gone at least partially bridezilla and insisted on some pretty high-budget items for her big day. For most people, wedding season is likely *the* most extravagant season of their entire lives, and the same was true for me.

The season of this book was undeniably an over-indulgent, luxurious, and ridiculous season of my life. I knew it at the time and tried to approach it with gratitude, and I am even more filled with awe now as I reflect back on my blessings. The constant travel, elaborate wedding trips, expensive clothes, and costly details of this wedding are not my day-to-day life, as much as I might sometimes wish it was. My day-to-day, as I'm writing this Author's Note, for example, mostly consists of manic late night drafting, early morning editing sessions, and somehow trying to do 500 things at once while my seven-month-old daughter may or may not nap for forty-five minutes or less. My life today is pretty much the opposite of self-indulgence, as I spend 99 percent of my time thinking about milk in one capacity or another. I'm currently still wearing a sweatshirt covered in baby food from my daughter's breakfast and mismatched sweatpants I am only now realizing are on inside out. It's admittedly a far cry from designer duds. And still, I know this won't last forever, either, so I'm soaking in the postpartum cocoon and snuggling my little meatball as much as I can between the to-do list items of my life. Like I said, every season is different.

All this to say, I acknowledge how unbelievably privileged my life is and I am appreciative beyond measure for the family, blessings, safety, and resources I have been afforded by the genetic lottery. I am aware the experiences I have had in my thirty-seven years on this earth are atypical, and I cannot even begin to express the depth of my gratitude.

As cringey as it sounds, I am not trying to brag or shove the opportunities I have been given in your face. But to tell this story in its entirety, I have to share the extravagant and sometimes ostentatious events of the wedding season.

So I hope you can read this memoir with the intention it was written. I simply tried to bring you along for the whole of the ride, gory and unflattering and yes, at times wasteful, details and all. I hope you can see this terrifying journey for what it was and understand it's not about the wealth or the dresses or the trips. It was never about the over-the-top wedding season, which is precisely why I didn't follow through with the it. I refused to choose the luxurious façade, blessing though it was, because I refused to prioritize something false over my own true happiness. I refused to choose anything over myself and my life. For that's what this story is really about: reclaiming my life, for me.

Reclaiming the life that went up in smoke.

Reclaiming a life that is authentic and filled with love.

Reclaiming my life that I have now built into one hell of a fabulous mess.

Nothing more, nothing less.

Introduction

In case you were not one of the 323 people invited to my wedding, or you thought it was a joke, or perhaps you misread the title of the book altogether, spoiler alert–I called off my wedding. I planned and fluffed and puffed my way through an entire year of wedding regalia, only to call it off two weeks before the fateful date. I saw what I thought was the finish line, and instead of "finishing strong," I walked away.

I walked away from the image of a perfect life I had so carefully constructed in my own mind. I walked away from the expertly crafted public image of Mr. Ex and me as the perfect couple–Barbie and Ken, Brad and Jen, Sandy and Danny–at least as far as Instagram was concerned. I walked away from what a respectable Oklahoma woman would do and made a choice I feared would embarrass my entire family.

Yet, in walking away from all of these things, I also walked away from a relationship that was flat out not meant for me. I walked away from settling. I walked away from a marriage that I knew deep within my soul was misaligned with the person I wanted to be.

And you know what, I am grateful. Every. Single. Day.

My story is filled with confusion, doubt, self-loathing, guilt, and pain. It has moments of sorrow and of despair, like the night I told Mr. Ex, "I do not want to marry you." Yet, it also has moments of self-examination, open conversations, reflections, growth, honesty, courage, hope, and even hilariously ridiculous anecdotes that are funny in hindsight but were more mortifying as they happened in real time–insert *Say Yes to The Dress* theme song here.

If you're hoping I can give you the answer to whether you should call your own wedding off, then you won't find a simple answer to that complex question here, either.

But, if you're hoping I will share honestly about what I was feeling, about the deep, resounding knowing I felt when I decided to call it all off, and the learning and growth I have been able to achieve since, then you're in luck. If you want to know what happened when I did the bridal unthinkable, the post-apocalyptic fallout, and all I've been through as the years have passed, stay tuned. And even if you want to skip to the hilarious, movie-worthy, cringing even as I type these bridal memories…then do I have a story for you.

This is *my* experience calling off a wedding and the hard truths I discovered in the process, yet it could just as easily be yours. Or perhaps your sister's, your aunt's, your friend's, your boss's, your barista's, or your best friend's sister's cousin's aunt's.

Need I go on?

Whether you realize it or not, everyone knows someone with a story like mine. Someone in your inner circle felt this way, for some reason felt compelled to dismiss it, and is now divorced or, perhaps worse, fundamentally unhappy in a life in which they feel trapped. Someone you randomly open up to at a coffee shop may have gone through the exact same thing after graduating from law school, and post-wedding call off, now shares two boys with another woman he has been happily married to for the last twenty-two years. If this sounds specific, it's because it's true.

Yet, for some reason, we refuse to talk about it.

We don't own our fears and share them with trusted friends. We don't prioritize ourselves. We don't admit the terrifying reality that sometimes we are about to marry the wrong person. We are so indoctrinated in believing a wedding–not even a marriage, mind you, but a wedding–is proof of a successful relationship that we take the plunge no matter what. Heaven forbid we have to wait a little bit longer than thirty years of age to find a deep, abiding, perfectly partnered love. Instead of celebrating the possibility of finding it one day, we live under a countdown, and NOT talking about it is only making the problem worse.

Now, I am not suggesting every person makes the wrong choice. But the point is, calling off a wedding is common. In fact, sources estimate that one in five engagements does not end in a wedding (Camisha), which means 20 percent of people swimming in en-fiancéed bliss will ultimately choose a different path. According to the National Diamond Syndicate, this equates to over half a million U.S. engagements a year that do not result in a wedding. Never mind the millions more who are simply in a relationship they wish to exit but haven't quite made it to the engagement phase yet.

So, you see, calling off a wedding is not an anomaly. Rather, it is a required act of bravery for some, and yet it remains taboo. Worse, it's painted as shameful.

Try Googling "calling off a wedding at the last minute" or "should I call off my wedding," and though you will see a few sparse blog posts, several Reddit threads, and even one article from *The Knot* (ironically, the mecca for all things pro-wedding planning), there are a shockingly small number of conversations happening about this topic.

In recent years, women in our society have managed to open up to one another about mental health issues, miscarriages, sexual abuse, and sexuality (gasp), in general. So why are we not also talking openly and honestly about calling off weddings and ending relationships not meant for us? What makes us so afraid to own these intense, albeit terrifying, feelings of doubt?

Honestly, it is different for every one of us.

This book is my attempt to finally bring my experience with the big, bad, bridal ugly into the light. It's my attempt to share my tears, my laughter, and the resulting growth and perspective I gained from one of the most formative seasons of my life.

It's my attempt to take away the mystery and the shame.

It's my truth about what happened when I called it off.

Yet, in the end, this is not just a "me" story–rather, it is a "we" story.

So without further ado, let's do this.

Part I
Once Upon A Time

"Fate sends us little signs, and it's how we read the signs
that determines whether we're happy or not."
– *Serendipity*

KATHERINE ROSE WOLLER

Chapter 1

Champagne Problems

"There is no choice more intensely personal, after all, than
whom you choose to marry; that choice tells us,
to a large extent, who you are."
– Elizabeth Gilbert, *Committed: A Love Story*

*Hi friend. I don't want to talk about details right now,
but I wanted to let you know that even though Mr.
Ex and I love each other, we have decided not to get
married. I'm so sorry for any inconvenience this
causes you. Thank you for supporting us.*

*R*ecord scratch.
Back up, back up, back up.
Who in the world is Mr. Ex, you ask?

Well, buckle up, Buttercup, because this is about to be a
wild ride.

It all started one glorious fall afternoon in Lower
Downtown Denver, aka LoDo. Gaggles of Sunday
Fundayers, myself and my friends included, queued up
outside the iconic day club, The ViewHouse, and waited
patiently to enter the hedonistic heaven out back. As soon
as we walked in, we saw the massive outdoor volleyball
court was already in full-on game mode. We looked for an

open daybed, but these epic loungers were already taken by those intent on getting a front row view of the overgrown man-children in action on the court.

Still, it was all pretty much perfect, and I'm not embarrassed to admit I spent MANY a Sunday afternoon playing volleyball in my club clothes, even joining in on a tug-o-war competition a time or two. It was pure joy for a late twenty-something who was just looking for a good time. I guess it's no surprise I found a very good looking, very good time in Mr. Ex there as well.

From the first moment Mr. Ex bumped into me (literally), I was in big trouble.

I heard his deep voice and velvet Georgia drawl exclaim, "Sorry, ma'am," from somewhere close behind me, and when I looked above his leanly muscled shoulders, there was an even-more-perfectly chiseled jawline. He was a dead ringer for Glen Powell circa 2022's *Top Gun: Maverick*, and my jaw may have actually hit the sticky bar floor. Even my forever wingman, The Ride or Die, knew something was happening. She's a tough, no bullshit, never hold back type of gal, and if stuff ever went sideways I know she would be sitting next to me in the slammer, rather than bailing me out the next day. She was that kind of friend, and she was there to witness this fateful meet-cute. She saw my eyes light up and a sly smile creep across my face as I protested with faux indignation, "Who you callin' ma'am, sir?"

Mr. Ex chuckled, his bright blue eyes sparkling with what I would learn was his signature mischievousness as he stared back unapologetically. We stood there, looking defiantly at each other until The Ride or Die grabbed my arm and dragged me away to where the rest of our friends were gathered.

She yelled over her shoulder at Mr. Ex, "Stay away from her–she's a sucker for guys like you!" as we walked to the other side of the court.

Game on.

You know how when you spot a super-hot guy at a bar or a club or a party, you can't help but find yourself scanning the room for him? Accidentally catching each other's eyes across the room and then cursing under your breath as you quickly look away, pretending you had been looking for a friend instead? Trying to be nonchalant and cool, but failing miserably? Well, that was me. And still, despite my deep and immediate attraction, I had zero intention of talking further to this handsome hunk of a man.

Mr. Ex had other plans. He not only had the audacity to continually catch my eye and smile, blatantly breaking rule number seventy-two of covert bar flirting, but he would sneakily find ways to creep up behind me and accidentally bump into me again, ON PURPOSE. I guess it's not really accidental if it's on purpose, but you get what I mean. I'd protest. The Ride or Die would guffaw, and we would move again, trying to avoid the inevitable.

Still, he finally wore my wing woman down and she resigned to letting us chat, but not without first letting me know this was "my own fault now."

I have zero recollection of what we talked about. Perhaps it was the vodka soda with lemon, carcass in, or perhaps it was the spell I was already falling under, but I do remember we exchanged names. No numbers, just a full name and secret hopes, at least on my part, he would somehow find me and reach out the next day.

I uttered a quick, "Welp, see ya later," as our party continued on elsewhere, floating down Market Street and onto the next bar, and that was the dreadfully anticlimactic end to our very first scene.

I guess I made an impression, because Mr. Ex did in fact reach out, via Facebook. He messaged me to say it was nice to meet me and after a few back-and-forths, he asked if a group of us should "hang out." Given that I was twenty-nine and no longer interested in the forced, awkward group-hang scenario of my younger, less mature dating days, I declined.

"Sorry, I'm not really interested in that," I wrote.

Mr. Ex countered, "What would you be interested in?" Smooth from the start.

"A proper date," I replied.

"I'd love to take you on a date, but I'm kinda seeing someone and it wouldn't be appropriate to also take you on a date." Credit to him for being honest.

"Then let me know when you are free to take me out. Until then, nice to meet you and have a good week."

That was it. Sayonara, sucker.

Despite my propensity for gorgeous men, I was so NOT interested in a taken man. Sure, I was openly disappointed as my Glen Powell look-a-like dreams of a few days ago were suddenly dashed. But alas, it was back to single-and-ready-to-mingle me.

As you have probably gathered, this was not the end of our story. Two weeks later, Mr. Ex slid back into my DMs and proclaimed we were going out on a proper date. Faith in my fantasy restored, I was thrilled and accepted his date immediately. The rest, as they say, is history.

Our meeting, at least, was straight up rom-com movie magic, y'all.

* * *

Let me quickly break down the next two years for you.

It started because he was gorgeous (see Glen Powell.)

I stayed because it was fun (see Glen Powell.)

Then, we upped the ante because his apartment fell through, and he needed a place to live. Well thought out it was not, so without thinking much about it, he moved in with me and we started building a home.

We fell deeply in love.

Mr. Ex continued his career in hospitality, and I doubled down on my professional goals as a marketer. I even went back to school at the University of Denver for my Master of Business Administration.

Life went on. We made more memories, some beautiful, some not.

The stakes kept getting higher, and the societal pressures got stronger.

My biological clock was ticking.

Despite the fact that we were truly incapable of bringing out the best in each other and mismatched in the things that matter most in a relationship–family goals, foundational beliefs, general life philosophies–we talked about marriage. Because sure, that makes complete sense.

Even though we had absolutely no business jumping into an engagement, after a lifetime of societal programming telling me I should get married and pop out 2.5 kids by twenty-five, I became singularly focused on getting engaged to my love before my sell-by date.

I was already thirty and therefore very much behind the ideal timeline to achieve what Kate Kennedy calls in her book, *One in a Millennial*, the Love-Marriage-Baby-Carriage Pipeline, or LMBCP for short. You know the playground nursery rhyme where the correct pattern of our lives is laid out in plain order? First comes love, then comes marriage, then comes baby in the baby carriage. That LMBCP was supposedly the ultimate goal for women, and I was getting closer every day.

We began looking at rings, and I'll admit I fully participated in picking out the exact stone for the engagement ring he purchased. I may not have known the precise date he was going to propose, but he showed me the ring the day he brought it home. So, unless he had some cruel trick planned instead, I obviously knew he was proposing soon.

I willingly participated in all of this, but in truth, I already wondered if we could go the distance.

You see, despite the love we shared, there are certain things I tolerated in our dating relationship that became more and more intolerable as casually dating moved closer to forever. I could choose to accept our toxic dynamic and certain behaviors that did not align with my personal values when it was just me in the picture. But when I began envisioning our life together with kiddos with perfect jawlines, my tolerance very quickly turned to fear. Sure, we loved each other, each in our own confusing, unhealthy, and sometimes destructive ways, but it was not the love of two souls destined to join their lives together.

It may sound harsh, but I think even Mr. Ex would admit it's true.

I say all this rather bluntly to paint a very clear picture of my emotional state for the events of June 12, 2018: the day Mr. Ex nervously, albeit handsomely, got down on one knee and asked the question that altered my life forever: *"Will you marry me?"*

CALLING IT OFF

* * *

For months, we had planned a proper Eurotrip, where I suspected the proposal was finally going to happen. Every detail was set to be perfect: the hotels, the activities, the outfits, heck, even the transit was all laid out beautifully. Well, I think you know what they say about best laid plans. In the interest of getting to the good part, I'll speedily retell the travel shenanigans with my very own verse to the tune of "I Am The Very Model of a Modern Major General" from *The Pirates of Penzance*.

Just kidding.

I actually did try to write my own version of this classic, but alas, only so many things rhyme with *hysterical*.

Anyhow, as we arrived in Paris, the city of love, I was ready for my own love story to commence. Apparently, Paris had other plans. After a national train strike totally screwed our peaceful transpo for "the big day," we frantically schlepped ourselves to the countryside of Reims, France, also known as the birthplace of what I will always refer to as *bubbles* and/or *champers* and/or the gloriousness that is champagne.

When I had a bit of a meltdown about the morning's snafus (not my proudest moment), Mr. Ex quietly walked away to calm his own nerves, willing me to relax as well. He just sat there in an antique, pastel pink armchair, tranquilly examining his hands. Not fidgeting, not clenching. Not doing anything really, while, like any 30-something woman in the midst of a crisis, I called my mom. Not with the unrealistic hopes she could change anything mind you, but simply because I really, really, really didn't want to take my crazy out on Mr. Ex.

Throughout it all, Mr. Ex was uncharacteristically calm. *Curious.*

Once in Reims, we checked into the most picturesque bed and breakfast I've ever seen, and we met our tour guide for the day, Thibault.

Thibault!

I mean, could you ask for a more perfectly poetic French tour guide than one named Thibault? Through my Katherine-Rose-colored glasses, it was kismet.

We spent the morning sipping rosé with bubbles so fine, delicate, and effervescent they really were a taste of the stars. As the vineyard tours continued, hint after hint confirmed that my "maybe this is finally it" engagement trip was actually a "holy smokes, I think he really is proposing *today*" trip. I was following Mr. Ex's breadcrumbs, and they were definitely leading to an altar.

Finally, after what I can only imagine was a tortuously long and arduous day of waiting, Mr. Ex's big moment arrived.

Our van slowed to a stop at the top of a hill in Ville-Dommange, and the view was breathtaking.

A lone oak stood tall above row after row of perfectly spaced vines, like a wise and caring king ever watchful of his kingdom below. Yet upon closer inspection, the vines weren't so perfect, after all. They were twisting and turning, writhing upwards as if sprinting toward the sun. At the far edge of the emerald sea stood the picturesque steeple of an ivory church. And though absolutely breathtaking, it filled me with thoughts of tradition–frozen and unyielding, foreboding even.

At the end of every other row was a ruby-red rose bush. As a temperamental flower, roses are the perfect first alert system, the watchdog of the vines, so to speak. You see, they succumb to bugs or fungus well before the grapes, and can therefore sound the alarm that something is brewing.

If there's something wrong with the roses, well then you, my friend, have a deep-rooted and unavoidable problem heading your way.

Perhaps I could have used my own internal rose bush to remind me of the trouble that had already begun in our relationship. Perhaps, as Katherine *Rose*, I was already both my own rosy guardian and the harbinger of tough times to come. Perhaps I always knew my truth.

With Thibault secretly filming away, Mr. Ex summoned me forward with his patented side-smile and a beckoning wave of his hand. I still have a photo of this exact moment– Mr. Ex looking expectantly and mischievously my way.

I sensed something was up. I followed him to the edge of the grapes, and he wrapped the muscled arm of his 6'4" frame around my shoulders, squeezing me in tight. I leaned my head into the crook of his arm, as we looked out over the sea of vines before us. The cool wind whipped at the hems of my trench coat and tousled my hair wildly; Mr. Ex took a step back and turned toward me.

Swiftly, he bent down on one knee and pulled a golden rose from his left, front jacket pocket.

I stumbled back in disbelief, bringing my hands to cover my face. Mr. Ex carefully opened the golden rose to reveal a hidden compartment containing the most brilliant pear-shaped diamond ring, which sparkled radiantly even on the gray and misty day.

He took my left hand, laughing, as he finished his long-rehearsed speech, and finally slipped the all-so-meaningful ring on my all-so-meaningful finger. He stood to embrace his new fiancée and we kissed quickly as he hugged me again, patting my back gently and beaming with pride. His shoulders relaxed after what must have been a huge rush of adrenaline, and he smiled, content.

All the while, my heart was racing like a herd of wild mustangs as I buried my head in the gap of Mr. Ex's jacket. Suddenly feeling unsure, I tried to hide my face, and my thoughts, in the ample fabric he wrapped snugly around me.

Even as it was happening, I knew something didn't feel right. Where before there was mostly just excitement at the fantasy, now there was also an inkling of fear. What's more, there was the shadow of perhaps the most insidious and destructive of all emotions: doubt.

What is wrong with me?! a voice whispered inside my now pounding head.

True, it was a monumental life moment to integrate.

True, there had been a lot of champers.

But truly, I knew it was more than nerves, and I was worried.

Is this all a mistake? I thought, even as we stood there hugging in the mist. *Is this meant for me?*

I had everything I thought I wanted, right in front of me: my champagne proposal.

And yet, I couldn't help but feel, well, *flat*.

There was something wrong with the rose, all right.

Chapter 2

The Glow I Left Behind

"Discontent is evidence that your imagination has not given up on you. It is still pressing, swelling, trying to get your attention by whispering: 'Not this.'"
– Glennon Doyle, *Untamed*

Wedding Countdown: Twelve months to go

Later that night we were back in our B&B, and I thought I'd be glad to have a minute alone. We both needed a break to decompress after the whirlwind of the day, but try as I might, I couldn't lean into it. I wanted to relax, but I couldn't. I was anxious, and instead of addressing the cause, I decided to stay busy, distract myself, maybe do something with my hands?

So, I took pictures of my stunning engagement ring. My ring with wine, my ring with the terracotta rooftops outside our third floor window, my ring with a yummy cheese plate, my ring in the rose, my ring on the bathroom counter. OK, so not all of them were keepers, but the light was actually pretty good in there.

When taking photos obviously did nothing to alleviate the stress, I jumped on the bed with Mr. Ex and said we needed to start telling our friends and family and therefore needed to make a list, first, because I love a list, and second, because it made sense to work methodically.

We contacted everyone on said "need to know before social media" list, until we agreed it was time for the moment where things finally get real: we posted it on Instagram. It killed a little time, and distracted me a bit, but it wasn't enough.

Still trying to hide from the nagging feeling in my gut, I abruptly told Mr. Ex it was time to go to dinner.

"Wait, now?" he asked tiredly and a bit disoriented from my rapid change of subject.

"Yes, now, we have reservations," I replied.

We had planned to have dinner at an enchanting spot in town, which I had secured after Googling the heck out of "most romantic places to eat in Reims." It should have been perfect. I assumed we would be excited, or at least hungry.

When he didn't immediately stand to leave, I asked, "What's wrong?"

"I'm just tired, Katherine. It's been a long day and I'd rather not go out. We've spent the whole day talking to people and I'm all talked out."

I'd like to report that I handled this graciously, but you can surmise I did not. After some solid bickering back and forth, we went to the restaurant, me practically towing him down the quaint cobblestone streets. At the moment, though, it didn't feel so quaint. We ordered a meal we never ate. We hardly uttered a word to each other across the candlelit table before both giving up completely.

Dejected, we paid the bill and high-tailed it out of there. I quite literally chased Mr. Ex through the most quintessentially romantic village ever as he strode swiftly away. Again, not the most romantic. Oh, the champagne problems of it all.

Back at the B&B, we silently and habitually washed our faces and crawled into bed. Both hurt, but also too tired to make a fight of it.

Now, I have enough guy friends to understand the unbearable weight of this day for Mr. Ex.

Looking back, I can understand why he wanted to relax and unwind privately. I totally get why he didn't want to feel like he had to put on more of a show. Even more so, I can now appreciate the fact that all he wanted to do was lay low with me.

I mean, come on, Katherine, of course he was exhausted! And if I had stopped for even one moment to steady myself, I would have realized how strung out and frazzled and fried I was, too. I was so hell-bent on pushing us forward for the sake of what we were "supposed to do on the day we got engaged" that I ignored how desperately he was pushing back for the simple chance to take a breath.

Neither one of us was wrong, per se.

Ok, that's a lie. I was wrong, but I was too wrapped up in avoiding my own uncertainty to see it.

It's true that you only get one chance to celebrate the day you got engaged, but the catch is this: there's actually not anything you are *supposed* to do. There were obviously things I thought we *should* do, but that's not the same. I was overcompensating and my doubts were making me frantic, childish, maybe even a little schizophrenic-ish, if that is a word. I was deeply conflicted, which only made me more confused, which in turn made me more conflicted...I think you get the picture. Clearly my frame of mind was panicky at best.

As we laid down for bed, I couldn't run or distract myself anymore. It had been one of the most emotionally heightened days of my life and still, I couldn't sleep. Instead, I finally started to notice those nagging, annoying misgivings in my head.

Perhaps I should have listened then.

But, as we all know, I didn't.

* * *

Fast forward eight long and confusing days to the Scottish village of Kirkoswald. New and epic surroundings, same miserable scene of a couple in distress.

Pardon my French, but I cannot put it any more frankly than this: we were fucking miserable.

Over the past week, we'd fought our way up and down the already moody streets of Edinburgh. We'd gotten along long enough to enjoy a few holes of golf, before tempers as strong as the Scottish winds blew through once again and blew up another should-have-been-magical day. We sat silently across from each other at quaint Scottish pubs that looked straight out Emily Brontë novels–if she had written about pubs, that is. We even fought about not having a TV in our room.

Rather than getting better as the trip went on, the pressure to "get it right" and the fights and the hurt feelings on both sides had only continued to fester.

Some of the arguments were silly (see TV fight above), and these were fine, normal even. A lot of couples differ in the ways they like to travel, and it can often lead to fights. But the way other arguments lingered and escalated was more concerning, reminding me of our legitimate red flags for the future. In those moments, I could not ignore the obvious truth–our differences didn't end with travel vibes.

We had different values, different definitions of a healthy relationship (both as individuals and as a couple), different beliefs about what it means to be loving partners, and different dreams for the future. In fact, we seemed to want different *lives* entirely, and I was not on board with *that* level of misalignment. I'd bet Mr. Ex probably wasn't excited for it, either.

It was a dream of an engagement trip, and yet we were both heartbreakingly unhappy, longing for a completely different reality.

So there I sat, devastated and confused in the center of our four-poster bed as we fought once again. It was our first night in the stunning cliff-side Culzean Castle, and instead of floating on cloud nine, we were distraught and exhausted from arguing incessantly through dinner. Looking back, I guess I don't really blame him for wanting to get the hell out of Dodge, but at the time, it just felt like Mr. Ex was determined to lean out. Like 4,374-miles-back-to-Denver out.

Alas, amidst tears on both sides, I was unwilling and unable to fight any longer. I sorrowfully conceded to Mr. Ex's plea and agreed to fly home early.

"Fine! You win, we can leave! We'll go home," I blurted out in frustration.

That was all it took.

Fight won, Mr. Ex calmed and went for a walk around the castle grounds while I changed our flights, canceled our remaining nights in Scotland, and fought to get refunds for the numerous activities I had planned during our happier moments.

I guess in some ways I always knew we would never be able to reconcile our dichotomous views on so, so, so very many facets of life. This trip, our first trip abroad together, only solidified it. Only ten-ish days into what was supposed to last forever, and some part of me was already wondering if I, too, needed to lean out.

Like Glennon Doyle wrote, *"Discontent is evidence that your imagination has not given up on you. It is still pressing, swelling, trying to get your attention by whispering: 'Not this.'"*

Not this, Katherine.

Not this, my imagination whispered in my mind.

It was the first time she spoke so boldly, but it wouldn't be the last.

From there, the doubts kept slithering in like the cold wind through the cracked stones of the castle walls around me. And as I clicked "Buy Now" on our next-day tickets home, the last flicker of our supposed engagement bliss was swiftly and permanently extinguished.

Welp, that didn't last long.

Chapter 3

The Giant Snowball of Doubt

"Follow your instincts. That's where true wisdom
manifests itself."

– Oprah Winfrey

For me, deciding to call off a wedding wasn't about one single incident. Instead, it was an accumulation of moments, little episodes and realizations each packing together into a truth I knew all along, growing slowly like a giant snowball of doubt.

Moments central to the wedding process, gone awry. Moments that showed how I was truly feeling. Moments where, when I finally started to examine what was happening, made it blindingly obvious what I would ultimately need to do.

Allow me to explain.

The doubts that accompanied me home from Scotland never left. Sure, I was able to push them aside for a while as Mr. Ex and I genuinely enjoyed being engaged at first. The initial celebration, the initial planning–it was all like a drug, really, and it relieved those doubts for a bit. But the closer we got to the wedding day, the faster the snowball of doubt rolled down my endless internal hill and the more I began to acknowledge the truth about our love.

Sometimes, the breakthrough moments were small, like when I sobbed in the front seat of a girlfriend's car as we waited out a spring rainstorm en route to the time-honored southern tradition: the Junior League Kitchen Tour. We were meant to be touring stunning home kitchens across Denver. But I found myself amidst two deluges that day, with my fears and doubts flowing right along with the rain.

Or when The Ride or Die—my lifelong best friend and the Thelma to my Louise—leaned across the aisle on our flight to my bachelorette weekend and asked if I wanted to get married. I waffled, she panicked. I didn't say I was fully *unhappy*, necessarily, but I wasn't overtly happy, either. It was guarded, but she saw right through my hesitation.

Or even more boldly when I told my mom how confused I had been mere moments before I was due at my first dress fitting. I must have truly scared the bejesus out of her, soaking my Earl Grey macaron and Ladurée latte as I wept openly on a park bench in Central Park.

I could go on, but I think you get the picture.

Reflecting back, I think these small admissions to friends and family, though often fueled by a little liquid courage, were my first baby steps in embracing the truth I had run from since the day we got engaged. Yes, there was a bit of external processing going on, but there was more to it. It wasn't exactly a plea for help, either, for I fully accepted I would be the one to make a choice one way or the other. Maybe there was a bit of hedging my bets, but ultimately, I think it just got to be too much to keep it all inside.

Like the snowball of doubt had grown too big to fit in just one body anymore.

I needed to confess said doubts, or risk being consumed by them.

However, given the fact that we were still very much engaged, this *was* a bit problematic.

* * *

At other times, the moments were more than just tearful confessions affecting me and me alone. Sometimes there was collateral damage I am still ashamed of. My bachelorette, for one, was an epically bad example of this.

Cue any and all pastel-fueled bachelorette scenes that take place in balmy ole' Charleston, South Carolina. After Mother Nature delayed my girlfriends with her hurricane force winds, I was left alone in C-Town for the entire first day of my bachelorette, and I will admit I was, how shall we put it, *unwell*.

To start, for someone who is already 90 percent convinced she shouldn't be getting married at all, having a low-level natural disaster occur during your bachelorette is a pretty obvious cosmic "STOP" sign. This sign, combined with the isolation, left me stewing in a whirl of emotions.

This was NOT cold feet. This was something else entirely, and though I tried to carry on when a few of the gals finally arrived, it was clear something was brewing.

I'll skip the gory details, but needless to say, bouncers don't love it when a thirty-something falls asleep at the best booth in the place. Long story short, we got kicked out of The Belmont on King Street because my friend took a nap. Classy, I know. Some nights you need to know when to call it, and this was undoubtedly one of those nights.

You know how sometimes, when you are well and truly pissed, you can actually *feel* your anger? Like a somatic wave riding up your spine, simultaneously giving you the chills and powering you up, whether you like it not? That was me. Despite my best efforts to breathe through it, I was seething. I was about to boil over, not with anger at my friend who made an innocent mistake, but with the stress of my own doubts and anger at myself as well. I tried to calm down, but I failed miserably.

As she profusely apologized for the hundredth time, something snapped inside.

I went full exorcist.

It was like the walls of my mental dam broke, and my anger came pouring out. Contorted in the front seat, I wheeled around to face my undeserving target, and I screamed, or perhaps screeched is more accurate, in one of those totally exasperated and beside myself voices where your yell is so rage-filled that it instantly gets hoarse and scratchy.

"ENOUGH! Enough!" I yelled as my friend cowered in the back, shocked into sobriety by the psycho I had become.

What a hot mess.

I let my intense anger at myself for not trusting my gut boil over, and I ruthlessly took it out on my beloved friend. I was battling too much, and she had somehow become the lightning rod for all of my frustration and fear. There's no other way to put it but this: I was an absolute ass. Even though I was truly battling my own demons, there is never an excuse good enough to justify acting this way. Consequently, and for good reason, I will forever be mortified by my actions. Even in the moment, I knew I was wrong. And I STILL couldn't stop the overflow of anger.

The next day, it was my turn to beg for forgiveness, and my friend graciously forgave me, even though I'm not sure

I deserved to be let off the hook so easily. Still, I was grateful for her grace, even when I was struggling to find it myself.

* * *

Then there was the true-blue bridal meltdown that kickstarted the snowball's momentum in the first place. The moment only two months after we got engaged where I should have hit pause but didn't.

Now this one, this one I have to tell in full.

Like many of us who were once little girls, I dreamed of and fantasized about and out-and-out planned my wedding for decades. Different eras of life equated to radically different wedding vibes; you name it, I planned it. I even began keeping clippings of all things bridal at the age of twenty-two, for crying out loud. I'm in my late thirties, so this was a P.P. era, people: Pre-Pinterest.

Fast forward ten years of planning and fantasizing about the perfect wedding and you can imagine the conflict I felt when it was finally time to hop on the plane to New York to search for THE dress.

On the one hand, it was a complete and total dream come true. It was such a blessing to fly to New York with my mom and best friends, and I was going to get to try on the most beautiful gowns I'd ever seen. This part was more than I could have ever asked for.

On the other hand, I was already pretty overwhelmed with doubt, and given the cold hard truth that I was not 100 percent sure I was marrying the right man, I wasn't convinced I could be 100 percent sure on the right dress, either.

This was the pressure-cooker that my mother, my maid-of-honor, The Ride or Die, and my other bestie, The Wild One–so named for her deluge of kinky curls and free-spirited nature–and I sauntered into as we deplaned our crack of dawn flight from Denver to Newark.

After two action-packed days of being stuffed, pulled, and pinned into dress after gorgeous dress, I still could not decide on THE dress. I mean sure, I was head over heels in love with the gowns, the design, the art. But I wasn't overwhelmed with a desire to walk down a long, all pink, flower-lined aisle to marry Mr. Ex in any one of them.

Instead, I kept saying I wanted "more."

They say hindsight is 20/20, and looking back now, it's painfully obvious as to why I couldn't pick a dress.

Every time I tried one on, something just felt off about it. I'd blame it on the straps, or the corset, or the fabric. I'd say I wanted more of this or more of that, but then I'd put on another gorgeous dress exactly like I'd described, and it would feel off, too.

As you've probably guessed, it wasn't about the dress–not really, anyway.

It wasn't that I wanted more of anything related to the dress.

I meant I wanted more of absolutely everything to do with my *relationship*.

I meant I wanted more alignment of our values, more unconditional companionship. More love. More of all the truly meaningful stuff in a partnership.

I meant I wanted more than the life I was currently living, and still, I blamed it on the dress.

Perhaps I should have quit while I was ahead, made a choice on any one of the beautiful bridal gowns I had donned in the past two days, and called off the search.

Or perhaps I should have trusted my gut when it said not only "more," but also "not this," just like it had whispered in Champagne just a few months before.

I don't know if I would have ever been strong enough to call it off then, but I wish I would have hit the pause button for long enough to allow myself a moment to think it all through.

For if I had paused, maybe I would have realized the need to take a step back. With space, maybe I could have reflected enough to embrace the truth. Who knows, maybe I really would have called it off earlier. If I did, I certainly would have saved both Mr. Ex and me from the months of agony that followed.

I also would have saved myself from experiencing what remains one of the most embarrassing, albeit hilarious now, moments of my entire life.

Alas, I was nowhere near secure enough to make such a monumental call. So, welcome to the episode I still refer to as the Great Kleinfeld's Dress Fiasco of 2018.

As soon as we walked in the door of the iconic New York bridal retailer, my skin was crawling with anxiety, like a million tiny ants running up and down my sweat covered limbs. This was August in New York, y'all, so it was H-O-T-T, hot.

There were nine or ten other brides in the lobby, and I swear I could feel each and every one of them sizing me up, judging whether or not I would be their biggest competition for a chance to be on the TV show that filmed there, *Say Yes To The Dress*.

I had absolutely no desire to be on camera in my current mental state, but they obviously did not know that.

We checked in, signed our filming waivers just in case, and looked around for a place to sit. There weren't any seats left, so we sat on the floor, in the corner, by the trash. It was a glamorous start.

Looking around, you could tell we were all a bit confused by this whole process. Ten nervous brides, ten opinionated mothers, ten-plus friends who didn't know the "right" thing to say. All of us waiting, until one-by-one a sales associate would emerge and call our names.

"Katherine," my gal said confidently as she looked around, perhaps hoping her client wasn't the one cowering on the floor by the trash bin.

Sorry, lady, I thought. *This just ain't gonna be your day.*

"That's me," I managed, as we awkwardly peeled ourselves off the floor.

She led us on a brief tour, giving an overview of the different styles on display as we answered the now standard pre-selection questions.

"Have you tried on dresses before?"

Yes.

"What styles have you liked?"

Anything that makes me look skinny.

"What is your wedding vibe?"

Modern Marie Antoinette meets pink, gold, and glamorous everything.

And so on and so forth.

Now let me be honest, I admit I like to dress up, but even then, I prefer an understated vibe. I can be uber-feminine, but mostly sport modern, European looks with the occasional cottagecore nod thrown in for variety.

Sometimes, I wear vintage rock shirts, white tanks, jeans, and snakeskin cowboy booties. In the summer, I hang out in all over floral maxi dresses with grandma cardigans. I do love the opportunity to sport a sexy cocktail dress, but not all-out, all-bling everything.

I love a theme and can certainly get carried away. But a modern Marie Antoinette vibe? This was much more Mr. Ex's wishes than my own and far beyond what felt authentic to me.

By this point, I was also tired of being forced into hot and heavy gowns. I was tired of analyzing my own appearance in the mirror with my perfectionism at an all-time high.

I was tired of the forced smiles and pageantry. I was tired of it all, really. Plus, as someone who struggles with social anxiety on the best of days, this entire public try-on situation was my own personal hell. Now that I think about it, such mental exhaustion is probably exactly how Mr. Ex felt the night we got engaged, but I digress.

Anyhow, my gal talked me into getting started with the trying-on process, and I was now sausaged into a fluffy, tulle gown with a gathered sweetheart neckline. With no more delaying the inevitable, my gal paraded me out into the bullpen as nine other brides emerged at roughly the same time. Dang, they had this show choreographed to perfection!

More ups and downs were exchanged by us all. More sideways glances from the entourages. More judgment. More internal conflict. More of it all as we each stepped on to our own personal pedestals scattered throughout the massive room.

Each of us was told to look directly at our reflections and ignore our friends and families. Each of us was secretly peering at one another like cotton-candy-clad warriors inspecting their opponents. Each of our families doing the same. Glancing, commenting, looking back again. Whispering comparisons at best, and insults at worst. If you thought high school girls were bad, let me tell you, brides and their entourages are far, far worse.

Atop my unwanted pedestal, I was once again asked, "So, what do you think?" as I tried but failed to explain my thoughts.

"Yes, it is beautiful, and comfortable, too. That's not the problem."

More questions.

"Sure, maybe a belt would help."

"No, I do not want to try it with a veil," I said assuredly, as one was thrust into my bridal-chic chignon anyway.

Then, there it was again: "I think I just want more."

"Perhaps we should try this," my New York Gal said, as she began to stuff my already huge skirt into a second full-skirted wedding dress, tucking in the bottom so only the skirt of the second and the corseted top of the first were visible.

I'll give it to her; it was a neat trick. The only problem was that I was now wearing two giant tulle straitjackets in a room that felt like it was well over a hundred degrees. I'm not entirely sure what it was about this exact moment that tipped me over the edge, but I suddenly felt my heartbeat quicken. Maybe it was the heat, or how I now felt physically trapped as well. My head started pounding and sweat careened down my back like someone had turned on a faucet under my dress. So much sweat that I instantly soaked through the first wedding dress and was steadily working my way through the second.

Oh, Lord, help me, I thought.

Then people began to gather, like looky-loos at a car crash. I'd like to think they sensed my discomfort and were there to offer aid, but when all they did was pair off into groups of two and begin to inspect, comment to each other, inspect, point, whisper, and inspect again, I knew there was no help in sight.

The women who I had so often seen on TV now turned their gaze upon me, and their presence filled me with dread.

Then a thought hit me like a ton of freaking bricks: *Holy moly. What if they put this on TV!?*

Feeling conflicted and confused internally is a totally different level of embarrassment than having a breakdown on national television. *Plus, what if I called it off? Would they have to issue a retraction? Would they put a small disclaimer at the bottom reading something like, "at the time this episode aired, this bride never made it down the aisle?"*

FML.

I fought desperately to hold back the tears suddenly welling up in my pale blue eyes, but I couldn't think of anything to say that might help me escape with my dignity intact. All I could think was, *NOT THIS.*

Not this dress.

Not this show.

Bloody hell, not this!

I had enough wherewithal to try to psych myself up before all hell broke loose, and I genuinely tried to summon the courage to speak up. I thought about sharing my doubts. I thought about pushing pause. But I. Just. Couldn't. Do. It. I wasn't ready. Whether I wasn't strong enough, or I didn't trust myself enough, or whether I was just so utterly embarrassed, I don't think anything would have made a difference at that moment.

In most scenarios, I like to think I'm pretty dang strong, perhaps a badass, even. But that day, I wasn't enough. I simply couldn't do it.

So instead, I wept.

"I'm just really overwhelmed," I sobbed aloud.

Which was true, even if only half of the real problem at hand.

"I'm so overwhelmed!" I whimpered again, realizing dejectedly that I was now ugly crying in the middle of Kleinfeld's.

Double FML.

Instantly, the "friendly" seamstresses scattered like cockroaches when the lights come on. Them suckers are quick.

So, I took a page right out of their playbook and ran away too. I don't mean I hurriedly made my way back to the dressing room. No, I mean I ran. Literally RAN right through the middle of the store. Now, I'm a lifelong athlete and an avid runner, so I truly fled the scene with the utmost speed and agility.

Gathering armfuls of tulle, I lifted the hems of my skirts and leapt off my pedestal like a ballerina in *Swan Lake*. In a massive, fluffy streak of white that only a woman in two wedding dresses could create, I bolted straight for the safety of the dressing room. My veil was flowing in the wind as two salesgirls actually chased me down screeching, "Get the veil," snatching at me as they ran. I briefly dipped my head back so they could take it away before I continued bobbing and weaving through dumbstruck mothers of the brides.

Still crying and still unbelievably overwhelmed, I pirouetted my way back to my own tiny dressing closet and slammed the door behind me.

I finally exhaled. Safe at last.

Or so I thought.

In an instant, the two gals who had chased me across the shop knocked frantically at the door. I loathed facing them, but, exhausted now that the adrenaline was receding, I resigned to let them in. Immediately and without asking, they stripped me down. This is not an exaggeration, folks! They literally peeled the dresses off my sweat-soaked body and left me standing there, stark naked, save the nude lace thong you are required to wear when trying on white.

No clothes, no protection, no façade. They must have taken pity on me for when they came back, they brought a massive floor fan into my room to try to cool the old girl off.

Somewhat catatonic at this point, I stood there swaying in time with the back and forth of my fan, like the tick of a depressing metronome.

Naked. Vulnerable. Striped in every sense of the word.

There was no hiding from the truth. I had nothing left. No more strength to make everyone believe I was a happy bride, and absolutely no clue what to do. I was standing there, completely raw, completely overwhelmed, and thinking to myself, *Not this, Katherine, not this.*

Blessedly, I do not remember how I got dressed or what the staff said when Mom, my besties, and I left.

I do remember a few hours later, though. My nerves were still frayed, but The Wild One convinced me to join her in the Plaza Food Hall for a piece of chocolate cake and a glass of the good stuff. I think she was desperately trying to somehow bake me back together with sugar and champs. God bless The Wild One, and chocolate.

As we chatted softly, she was not overly positive, and she did not assert that everything would be perfect. Instead, she was real, and she was supportive.

She asked if everything was ok with me and Mr. Ex and if there was anything I wanted to talk about. She asked all the right questions I should have answered honestly then and there. But given that I still wasn't sure what it was I *did* want, I couldn't bring myself to say I was realizing more and more that I *didn't* want to get married.

I was not yet ready to admit I was already having serious doubts. And though I had acknowledged deep inside how unhappy I was with the path I was heading down, I couldn't bring myself to share the burden of those doubts with others. I was not yet willing to trust my gut, so I lied. I lied to my best friend's face.

"I'm fine," I heard myself say. "I think I'm just tired and ready to go home."

I was so convincing I almost believed myself. Almost.

For in the end, it was not up to The Wild One to save me, or anyone else, for that matter. I was the one who would have to step up, put my big-girl nude lace thong on, and step off the runaway wedding train. I was the one who would have to FINALLY listen to what I had known all along.

I was the one who would have to make a choice.

If I wanted something more from my relationship, from my life, then somehow I would have to embrace my giant snowball of doubt and save my dang self.

Chapter 4

Spiraling

"Trust yourself. You know more
than you think you do."

– Benjamin Spock

Wedding Countdown: Eight months to go
As you can probably guess from the title of this chapter, things took a bit of a downhill turn in the months leading up to the wedding. Beginning some time in the fall, call it November, I noticed a concerning pattern was emerging, and I'll admit upfront that it wasn't a good look.

I don't love airing my dirty laundry this way, but I feel it's important to show my humanness in all its fallibility. Could I have handled this season of life with more grace? Yes. Should I have taken my confusion out on Mr. Ex in this way? No. Were we both still very much in the wrong? Heck yes. At least that's my opinion, but I'll let you decide for yourselves.

As a chronic overachiever who based a good bit of my self-worth on accomplishments and success, it's no surprise I had a lot on my plate during this time. I was consulting on some small marketing projects after leaving my most recent corporate role, was knee-deep in studies for my MBA, and still heavily involved in leadership for the Junior League of

Denver's annual fundraising gala. I was juggling a lot professionally, plus trying to plan a wedding at the Broadmoor in Colorado Springs, Colorado, with the help of Mom and the Wedding Planner Extraordinaire. And yet, clearly, I was dropping balls left and right.

For one, I was not prioritizing my health and well-being at all and had let my regular workouts fall completely by the wayside. Also, I was definitely not focusing on finding more permanent job opportunities, post-graduation. Even the wedding planning was more haphazard than I would have liked, at least on my end, though I think you can understand why this piece was challenging.

To make matters worse, night after night, I'd try anything to escape the conflict in my mind and justify that I deserved a drink. I was too sullen to cook, so I would indulge in a "wine for dinner" night in. I made the excuse that it wasn't really problematic, since it's not like I was going anywhere. Plus, I was pretty depressed by this point, so a next-day hangover pretty much fit the tone of my daily mood. I was justifying my drinking left and right, and even though I was disappointing myself with my obviously self-destructive behavior and lack of focus, I was desperate for a little numbing out. Let me be clear, Mr. Ex had vices of his own, but even so, he was less than enthused about this development.

Typically, the scene played out like this...

I had a favorite hoodie at the time (OK, it's still my favorite) that was more than a wardrobe staple: it was literally the only item of clothing I wore around the house during those months. It was a red and black buffalo plaid zip-up sweatshirt with a peeling X-Games logo on the left breast. It was super faded, so the black was now gray, and the fabric was threadbare as all get out. It was my well-loved comfort blanket.

I bought said hoodie when I was a sophomore in college and proceeded to use it as my drunken safety blanket even then. Back then, I was supposedly living the college girl's dream, and yet for a variety of reasons I won't go into right now, I experienced a very big downward spiral of what felt an awful lot like depression, over-indulging, and generally looking for validation in all of the wrong places. I was averaging attending about two out of ten classes per week, and even though I was miraculously still making A's, I would avoid my classes by sitting at home and drinking on the couch, watching rerun after rerun of *Sex and the City*.

Sometimes I would cuddle with my roommate, but more often than not, I would stay up alone to drink. Some nights it was so bad that I would pop an Eggo waffle in our not-safe-for-dorm-room toaster oven, only to wake up the next morning to an unrecognizable black Eggo puck, thankful I hadn't burned the building down, all the while wearing my trusted X Games sweatshirt. Now, over a decade later, I was once again reverting to the exact same unhealthy coping devices without even realizing it. Despite having infinitely more responsibilities, I fell into the exact same pattern of behavior I used when I was at one of the lowest and most destructive and most depressed times in my entire life. Red flag, anyone?

I digress.

Each night, I would zip up my hoodie, flip the hood up over my sopping wet, post-shower hair, and head to the fridge. Selecting the flavor of the night, I would open a bottle of delicious white wine and fill my glass to the brim.

Satisfied with my HBP (half-bottle pour), I'd walk the ten yards back to the caramel brown leather couch that served as my own personal zone of safety within my home. Securely on my deserted island, wine in hand, I vegged out for hours watching garbage TV. Are you sensing a theme here?

By the time Mr. Ex came upstairs from his basement lair, I would be properly tipsy.

His footsteps would stop before he even reached the top stair, and a huge sigh would escape his lips. *Oof*, the disdain he could emanate with even one sigh and a glare my way.

I can only imagine what he must have thought in those moments. I mean, he wasn't the picture of a perfectly healthy lifestyle himself, but here I was, his future wife, drunk, curled in a ball on the couch, looking like a wet rat.

Emotionally raw, it was only a matter of time before we would slide into what a dear friend of mine calls the "negative context loop of doom." Each of us would bring out the absolute worst in the other, and reinforce bad behavior after bad behavior, back and forth in an endless spiral. In those days, we seemed incapable of being kind to one another, so the feedback loop wore on indefinitely.

Wine in hand, I'd turn to him and ask, "What?" in my most exasperated tone of voice, trying to match his level of contempt.

"I don't know why you're drinking so much wine on a random Tuesday night. Have you even eaten?" he would ask, half concerned, half disgusted.

"Tonight is a wine-for-dinner kind of night," I'd respond sarcastically, lifting my almost-empty glass in a mock cheers motion to no one and looking back at him only to give a sly nod of my head as if to say, "try me."

He'd scoff, unphased, and stare back hostilely at the sad silhouette I cut on the couch.

Some nights Mr. Ex would adhere to the well-known rule that you can't argue with crazy (or drunk), and retreat, no doubt confused at how we got to this point. He would huff and about face back downstairs to the media room, where he would put on his headphones, smoke a bowl, and resume playing Fortnite. It was his own attempt to escape from our miserable home life.

Once he was gone, I'd snuggle promptly back on the couch and try with all my might to hold the tears at bay. I may have acted tough, but I was fragile and raw in those days. I'd watch more trash TV and wrap the comforting blanket of numbness around my weary body, hoping to hide from my doubts, even if just for an hour.

Sometimes it would end there, and I would eventually crawl down to bed to sleep it off. Sometimes it escalated into arguments that threatened to rip my heart in two.

As the months ticked by and we marched ever so slowly toward our wedding, the perpetual arguments degraded us more and more. Somehow, they took a relationship that was already unhealthy and made it into something even less salvageable. It became even less aligned and less filled with love, and thus even farther from the authentic, forever partnership I craved.

Looking back now, I can admit that Mr. Ex absolutely had a point. He was totally and completely justified in trying to reign his floundering wine-drunk fiancée back in; it was his methods that were questionable. He may not have known what was causing me to act so out of character, but he knew it was a bad omen. And still, he never asked what was at the root of the change. True, it was not his job to read my mind, but I wonder if he suspected what was coming even then? I mean, I couldn't express exactly what it was at the time, but some very real part of me knew it was all completely wrong.

And still, I stayed silent.

Only my silence didn't make it better. It made it worse, widening the gap between my current reality and the dream I had for my future.

I'll admit it's possible I was trying to push Mr. Ex to the brink, hoping maybe if I acted bad enough, maybe he would call it off first. Not consciously, mind you, but some part of me kept pushing him away, knowing full well it was hurting him in the process. Like I said, we were both culpable here, and I won't deny that.

I slowly tried to break us from the inside out, until one night the urge to break free got a little bolder.

* * *

Wedding Countdown: Three months to go

In the months leading up to the wedding, I continued drinking more than usual as I tried to quiet the doubts in my head. For the most part, I kept this behavior confined to my own home, but as we crept closer to the big day, things got a little, how do you say, messy.

I don't even remember who I had gone out with, but I know the night was a doozy. I Ubered home and as the nondescript car drove away, I couldn't bring myself to go inside. My feet were frozen to the bottom step of the patio stairs and my body refused to move.

Then, flight mode kicked in hard.

I did an abrupt about face and walked a few houses down the road to sit on my neighbor's stoop. I could have sat on my own stoop, I guess, but I needed space to think.

It was unseasonably cold for a March night in Denver, but I didn't care. Perhaps freezing to death was better than walking back into what had come to feel like the warm and cozy prison of my life.

It was after midnight, and Mr. Ex was both worried about my well-being and pissed I still wasn't home. Again, understandable. We shared locations in those days, so he was able to find me with ease. He stormed out of the house and up the street to get me, closing the half block between us in only a few strides. He grabbed my arm and began to drag me back to our bungalow as we whisper-yelled at each other in the middle of our family-friendly neighborhood. Slowly and embarrassingly we made our way back to the house, despite my best efforts to free my arm from his grip. This part wasn't so understandable, in my opinion.

I was drunk and indignant. He was furious. It was a TERRIBLE combination.

The second the front door closed, all pretenses dropped away, and a slurry of insults, blame, tears, and name-calling swirled through our home like a tornado in the Oklahoma spring. We yelled and argued until I was so hoarse I no longer recognized the voice screaming from my lips. Then finally, exhausted, I blurted out the one thing I hoped would stop the fight:

"Well, maybe we shouldn't get married then."

There it was–the doubt I had been running from. She finally had a name. She hung in the silent air like a half-deflated helium balloon. And I was right. The fighting stopped.

Sometimes I still wonder what it was about this moment that finally pushed me to be honest.

Let's be real, the tipsiness had already removed my filter, so that didn't hurt. But there was something more. I was so fed up with our negative nightly cycle of toxicity, I was willing to say anything to interrupt it. Not only did I hate the way I was acting, but I was also genuinely done with Mr. Ex's demons and their impact on our life, too.

In therapy, we had worked tirelessly to learn healthy communication and somehow get on the same page for our future, but our irreconcilable differences remained. I was also exhausted and increasingly worried by the thought that this would be my forever. So, I was finally willing to try out the one phrase that would quite literally set me free from the engagement entirely.

Just a few simple words, and I could walk away.

So, I said it.

I said it to see Mr. Ex's reaction, and some part of me was in fact hoping it would stick.

Some part of me hoped I could wake up the next day and start the unplanning right then and there. But some part of me was still too ashamed to follow through. My logical, perfectionist, deeply indoctrinated good wife-to-be still wasn't ready, and unfortunately, she was still very much in control.

When I awoke the next morning, I panicked. Like I said, I wasn't yet strong enough to choose myself, and I wasn't ready to face the repercussions of what calling it off would mean. So, I did what many people do the morning after a late night fight: I followed Jamie Foxx's advice to "Blame It" all on the booze.

I backpedaled, hard, and pleaded for Mr. Ex's forgiveness.

I went on a full-on apology tour. I said I loved him. I said I was drunk, I was sorry, and I didn't mean it. I said all the things a loved one does when they are trying to reinstate the status quo. And still, I think we both knew on some level I meant what I said: maybe we shouldn't get married.

From that night on, I didn't sleep more than a few hours a night. I couldn't shake a nagging and persistent headache as my internal emotional pain had finally turned physical. I couldn't outrun my doubts, and yet, I wasn't brave enough to claim them yet either.

I wasn't ready to choose myself and fight for what I knew I deserved. I'm not even sure I knew what it looked like yet.

I wasn't ready to face the shame of other peoples' judgments of my bridal failings.

I wasn't ready to hope for the good that might be on the other side of all this fear.

And so… I spiraled on.

Chapter 5

The Fates Knew All Along

"Only do what your heart tells you."
— Diana, Princess of Wales

Wedding Countdown: Two months to go

Three women walked into a bar. One was married. One was engaged. One was single and ready to mingle. No, this is not the start to a bad joke. It is the start, however, to a rather defining moment in this whole saga—the moment I stopped running from my doubts.

Dressed to the nines in the dungeony dark of Lafitte's Blacksmith Shop Bar, one of the oldest, and in my opinion coolest, dive bars in New Orleans, The Single Lady, my long-time Denver lady friend, The Wild One, and I sucked down a few frozen cocktails in the blink of a heavily lined, smokey eye.

We swayed to the jazzy rhythms, unselfconscious and totally free in the way women often dance with each other, but almost never do with men. The bourbon, the sticky NoLa heat, the magic of the city: something was in the air.

As I turned around, there was an unknown man staring at me through the crowd.

Tall, dark, handsome, and with eyes so dark they burned right through me, his expression appeared as if he knew me, but that was impossible. I had no idea who this fellow was and yet I was transfixed, staring curiously back at this human who stopped me in my tracks.

A squeal of excitement escaped from somewhere to my left and I was knocked back down to reality as The Single Lady bumped my shoulder in her hurry to greet her new acquaintances.

Imagine my surprise when she walked right back to the man who was still standing there waiting for my gaze to return to his.

A sly smile of recognition finally broke his stone façade and I couldn't help but throw my head back and laugh. Of course she knew the man I will forever refer to as Mr. New Orleans.

Apparently, The Single Lady, being the gregarious, confident boss she is, made friends on her short flight to the Big Easy. She wined and dined these gentlemen en route and convinced them to meet us at Lafitte's to celebrate her birthday weekend with us.

I made my way over to our now mixed group and extended my hand. Saving the best for last, I braced myself as I finally turned to Mr. New Orleans. A warm handshake matched the gentle nod of my head, and as we locked eyes I uttered, "Nice to meet you." Innocent by all outward accounts, but inside…well, inside I felt an instant pull.

Stunned, I quickly pulled my hand away, subtly flexing away the tension lingering on my fingertips.

"Who's up for a nightcap?!" I exclaimed cheerfully, hoping my sudden burst of bubbly energy would redirect us all.

The night continued mostly as you would expect, with the six of us wandering around the French Quarter, bar hopping, singing along with the bluesy street performers, and just generally enjoying a carefree night in the Big Easy.

As closing time rang out, we said our *au revoirs*.

Mr. New Orleans bid me *adieu* with a quick brush of his lips to my outstretched hand. With the smallest whisper of lip to skin, he was gone for what I assumed would be forever. "So Long, Farewell," to you sir.

The Wild One, The Single Lady, and I waded through the humid swamp of Bourbon Street as we walked lazily back to our Airbnb. Breathing a deep sigh of satisfaction, we plopped on the couch at home. Spontaneously, we broke into the knowing laughter of longtime girlfriends who had just had a truly epic night. For me, it had been a welcome respite from the chaos and turmoil back home.

Coming down from my post-girls-night high, I slipped into my coziest sweatpants and thought wistfully, *What a night*, as the warmth of our girls' trip continued to envelop me.

But lying in bed that night, my head was spinning, and not from the multiple Hurricanes I'd consumed earlier that evening. Instead, I couldn't shake the thought of this mysterious human with whom I felt bizarrely pulled. Mr. New Orleans, with his cool but intense demeanor, had been the perfect gentleman to match my southern lady, and yet something lingered, like the smell of a delicious perfume.

Something about his look, those eyes, the instant pull.

Something inside me was not yet ready to let go.

I was confused even then as to how I was so drawn to someone who wasn't Mr. Ex, and it quite frankly scared the heck out of me. Yes, we had been in a bad place for months on end, but it was unlike me to feel an immediate connection like this with anyone. Instant lust, sure, but this was different. It felt like we somehow knew each other, like I could trust him. Like maybe I could even be honest with him as I was desperately trying to be honest with myself.

Maybe there was something to this connection after all, I thought as I drifted off to sleep.

The next morning, we headed out to take part in one of the most iconic experiences that NoLa has to offer: a tarot card reading! We were all giddy at the prospect of a "real" psychic reading, and though I have since dove headfirst into the world of mediums, natal chart readings, Reiki, and the like, at the time, I was a psychic virgin.

Our trio walked to the edge of the French Quarter where we entered a hole-in-the-wall mysticism shop, similar to those you might find on any corner in this enigmatic town. Candles of every size, shape, saint, or purpose; incense, talismans, beads, crystals–you name it, they sold it.

We checked in with the gal behind the cashier's desk– we had made advanced appointments, after all–and then wandered around aimlessly, trying to look comfortable even when we were so clearly out of our element.

Finally, out glided Madame Mystical.

Round, raven-haired, and dressed in a perfectly flowy ensemble that looked appropriately tarot-cardy, she came toward me.

"You must be Katherine," she said in a breathy whisper.

Dark plum turban atop her head and bangles upon bangles tinkling on her arms, she parted the curtains and beckoned me forward with a kind, but firm, "Right this way."

We entered a small space at the front of the shop, just big enough for a tiny card table and two stools, surrounded with heavy black tapestries. It didn't seem super private, but after stepping in and drawing the fabric around us, it was indeed enough to muffle all traces of the bustling city outside.

Maybe it was a spell, but as she closed the curtains around us, we were suddenly very alone.

Maybe this makeshift chamber really was a portal to the future, however daunting that was.

Madame Mystical certainly did know how to set the stage.

As she shuffled her well-worn deck of tarot cards, she went through her undoubtedly standard spiel. This deck is blah blah blah, we will pick three cards, yada yada yada. You know the drill. Then she asked the question I was anticipating: "What do you want to see today?"

As a doubt-riddled bride-to-be, I naturally asked about my love life. I mean what else would I have asked about at that point in my own personal saga? I was less than two months from a wedding I was more and more certain I didn't want, and yet I was still dutifully walking the plank, preparing to take the plunge.

She nodded, as if this was the question she had expected and took a deep breath in before turning over the cards. The first card hit the table with a *thwack* as she dramatically released the corners.

Then the next. *Thwack.*

Then the third.

Each card stared face up as she surveyed the damage without so much as an inkling of meaning crossing her face.

Thwack. Thwack. Thwack.

Three more cards, and still she gave away nothing. It was maddening.

Madame Mystical would make one hell of a poker player, I thought.

Thwack.

She placed the deck gently to the side and looked up to deliver my fate.

It's funny, really, for I can't remember a single card she pulled that day. Not one. But despite my inability to recall a King of Cups or Queen of Bourbons (yes, I know there's *not* actually a suit of Bourbons), you can be damn sure I remember the gist of her message.

In short, the cards foretold the truth I had been hiding from for months: my current relationship was not meant for me.

Thwack.

She continued. It seemed my future did hold another love–a stable, morally-aligned, supportive partner. Someone who would be my best friend, my adventure buddy, equally curious, my constant companion with whom I would laugh endlessly.

My future king.

My as yet unmet (of this she was certain) other half.

In short, a future love so great it would transform my life for the better–transform me for the better.

The only problem was, I hadn't met this mystery man yet and she could not tell me how long it would take until I did.

I was intrigued with this divination of a someday true love–I mean who wouldn't be? But, I set that aside.

The more pressing issue was the fact that this prophecy was decidedly not referencing a happily ever after with Mr. Ex.

Thwack.

Now, I took all of this information with a giant grain of salt, as I do not put much stock in tarot card readings from gals in touristy mystic shops. No offense to Madame Mystical. Even so…though I didn't believe this was cosmic confirmation that today was the day to call off my wedding, I did listen to the voice inside saying bluntly, "She has a point."

Shaken up, I needed to get some fresh air, and immediately told the gals I was going for a walk. My friends looked on, concerned by the sudden shift in my energy, but bless their hearts, they let me go my own way in peace.

Spiraling once again, I walked to the antique market across the street. Trying to push the prophecy from my mind, I browsed the tables haphazardly, only half-seeing the stalls lined up in front of me until one particular vendor caught my eye. Vintage books!

It's always the books for me, I thought, as I rushed toward what I knew would be the salve to soothe my aching soul.

Title after serendipitous title spoke to some small piece of me, sending me messages of reassurance and guidance. Yet, it was a nearly impossible choice. In the end, I went for something light and harmless.

Vintage cookbook in hand, I walked the few blocks to Jackson Square and sat solo on a park bench. I read recipe after recipe of proper southern comfort food, each one filling me back up to face the reality of my life, feeding my soul just enough to face my doubts head on.

Chicken soup for my bridal soul perhaps?

Satiated, I strolled back toward the girls.

After all, I couldn't wait to hear their futures so I could conveniently avoid talking about mine.

It appears the Unstoppable Force of the universe had other plans.

Gazing down at the tattered cover of my new tome, I turned the corner and bumped smack into an Immovable Object.

There he was again, with his onyx eyes staring profoundly into my soul and a brow so furrowed it would make Heathcliff look cheerful: Mr. New Orleans himself.

"You again," I whispered, half irritated, half excited.

"Were you hoping for someone else?" he chuckled.

Still a bit raw from my reading, all I could manage was an honest apology.

"I'm sorry, it's just been a really confusing day, and I don't have the energy for this," I said as I gesticulated broadly, waving my hands in the general direction of his face.

Instantaneously, his demeanor changed. His hard edges and an air as cool as stone were suddenly replaced with tenderness, compassion, and genuine concern. His smile melted away as he softly gazed my way and offered a lifeline with one simple phrase.

"Are you OK?" he asked.

A totally harmless question. One I had been asked hundreds upon hundreds of times in the preceding months, and yet this time, for the first time, I didn't feel like I had to hold anything back.

"No, I'm not," I started.

But it didn't end there. The words kept tumbling out in an uninterrupted deluge of self-disclosure. Heavy, fast, and unrelenting, my monologue rolled on. I shared my fears about Mr. Ex and our potential future. I shared the story of our shining engagement followed by the reality check of our engagement trip. I shared the endless fights we had since and my drunken half-confessions to family and friends. I shared my deep internal conflict and the doubts that never left me alone.

I shared the details of what was supposed to be our perfect wedding, and the reality that I was certain we would never have a perfect marriage.

I told him all of my darkest secrets and was too tired to be ashamed of any of it.

So, I continued.

I told him my biggest passions in life and what I dreamed of at night. I told him of the life partner I wanted and admitted it didn't feel possible with Mr. Ex.

I told him everything. Every last bit.

I laid it all out, right there on the cobblestones of Decatur Street.

I was done running from my doubts.

Naked and exposed, I peered up just enough to see how he would react to my now several minutes long rant.

He laid a gentle hand on mine, and with what felt like total and complete understanding, he replied, "I know."

Now, I don't think he *knew* knew all the details and ins and outs of my situation. He wasn't a psychic like Madame Mystical after all. But I do think he sensed how I felt and therefore "knew" the struggle I was going through. For one reason or another, I could feel we were connected. And I'd like to think the universe or God or higher power or whatever it is you personally believe in put him in my path precisely so he could bear witness to my truth.

I needed someone who could share the burden of my doubts.

I needed a shoulder to cry on where I wasn't worried about said person then turning around and judging me for it.

I needed someone who didn't really know me in my real life, and therefore didn't have all these preset expectations of me, who could just honestly and openly let me be me. Warts and all.

Here was this man, with his simultaneous intensity and quiet assurance, who seemed content to hold space for me to process. What's more, he seemed to somehow embrace my messiness and imperfection.

He didn't ask for anything in return, at least not then, and whether it was right or wrong, I almost instantly came to rely on him as my sounding board.

One massive confession on the streets of New Orleans.

One moment of undeniable honesty and I knew I wanted his friendship to last beyond the weekend.

After what turned out to be a rather emotional girls' weekend, it was finally time to head home. The Single Lady and I Ubered to the airport to catch our early morning flights, and as we sailed through the still-darkened streets, I waffled back and forth with what to do next. I had a text to Mr. New Orleans all queued up, but as my finger hovered over the send arrow, The Single Lady gave me a sound warning.

"Don't do it. You're playing with fire with that one," she said.

She was right. I knew texting someone other than my fiancé was a bad idea. I knew it wasn't the right or kind or honest thing to do.

But I also knew something about Mr. New Orleans was helping me face my doubts. Somehow, his quiet strength was already helping me to remember how strong I was in my own right, and it had only been one day.

So, even though I knew it was wrong, I hit send.

"Really glad we met you all. Safe travels and keep in touch."

That was it.

One text. One text and I knew I had crossed a line.

One text, and then another, and then another as Mr. New Orleans and I stayed in touch for weeks to come. Me sharing openly about my relationship in a way I couldn't with anyone else, him providing solace and validation.

Trust me, I don't relish sharing my shortcomings with the world and I know admitting this makes me look like the villain in this situation. Obviously, I am not proud of how I handled myself. But, I'm willing to put my own faults out there so maybe you feel slightly less alone in whatever far-from-perfect moments you may be dealing with, too. You don't have to be perfect to call off a wedding. In fact, maybe it's more honest if we all just admit we aren't perfect. To err is human, and even in all of my obvious fallibility, I'm not the only culpable party here, and I think you know that.

For that matter, I could very easily have left this part out of the book entirely, and maybe I should have. But if I didn't share this piece of the story, then I wouldn't be able to explain how much it helped. For I'm not entirely sure I would have had the courage to call it off if it weren't for these truthful conversations.

Looking back, I think the universe knew I needed a push. It knew I needed a little extra something, and so it sent reinforcements in the form of Mr. New Orleans. It sent me a tool, a mirror if you will, so I could finally see myself clearly.

Over time, our chats reminded me more and more that I was actually in control of my own fate all along. That even though Mr. Ex and I were planning forever, and everyone expected us to follow through with said plan, I was still the one who could decide if this was the life I wanted to lead. I was the one who had to live with my choices, and ultimately the only opinion that mattered was mine. Quite simply, I had to stop betraying myself.

For if I didn't put myself first, then who the heck would?

Thwack.

Chapter 6

Therapy

"Be patient and tough;
someday this pain will be useful to you."

– Ovid

Wedding Countdown: Two months to go
Amidst all the fighting and spiraling and doubting (oh my), I want to take a minute, well, chapter, really, to discuss a very special person in my life, my therapist.

I. Love. Therapy.

Like, a lot a lot.

I am a life-long believer in therapy, so just for good measure, I'll say it again…*I love therapy.*

In fact, I love therapy so much that, to borrow a term the journalist and author Johann Hari used on a podcast with Elise Loehnen, I've been in "industrial strength therapy" for most of my adult life.

Allow me to explain. My parents divorced when I was five, so I'm not ashamed to admit that I necessitated fairly regular therapy sessions from a pretty young age. Perhaps this is why I don't subscribe to the stigma often attached to therapy, so much so that I majored in psychology for my undergraduate degree and even briefly pondered a career in child psychology. This was not my ultimate calling, but the practice of self-reflection and emotional self-care have remained a HUGE part of my journey with mental health through the last three-plus decades.

Your mind, like your body, needs as many positive habits as possible to function properly in today's social media-fueled, competitive, comparative, fast-paced, instant gratification-to-the-max world. So, to me, regular therapy sessions, daily gratitude journaling, and meditation are all integral facets of my commitment to a healthy lifestyle.

Furthermore, not only is therapy an incredible support during challenging life moments, it is also an equally invaluable tool during the high-flying good times as well.

Having someone in your corner who already knows you, your story, and in my case, your numerous neuroses (eek), makes the surprise obstacles we all encounter far easier to overcome, just as it helps to fortify and build your emotional capacity if practiced proactively.

This is why with every cross-country move, and there have been many, one of the very first calls I make is to secure a new therapist.

Upon moving to Denver in July 2012, I promptly asked friends for recommendations, Googled who was within walking distance of my Lower Downtown studio apartment, and booked several introductory appointments with a variety of local providers. I was determined to find the right fit for me and approached it a bit like speed-dating: efficient, to the point, and hopefully a successful matchmaking effort in the end.

From my very first "getting to know you" appointment, The Trusty Therapist, aka "my emotional support guide," and I clicked.

She was kind, warm, and intelligent, yet firm and certainly no nonsense. Most importantly, I knew I couldn't lie to her, which so many people do in therapy, despite the fact that lying in therapy is truly the antithesis of the whole point.

Anyway, the gist is, I liked her.

We connected, and I knew she would be my partner in mental health for the foreseeable future.

The Trusty Therapist saw me through a few different failed relationships early on in our partnership, so by the time Mr. Ex came along, she already knew me well.

She knew what made me tick, knew my shortcomings, knew my tendencies in relationships, my dating patterns, and she also saw the hard-fought growth I made through my mid to late twenties. I like to think we trusted each other, and I respected her opinion wholeheartedly.

Jump ahead to the season of my engagement and things got a bit...trickier...shall we say.

As I stated before, you can't, or shouldn't, lie to your therapist. They are the one place you can divulge all the things without fear of judgment, repercussions, or regret. And they require the whole truth and nothing but the truth if they are to help you effectively.

Fighting with your fiancé for any and all manner of things? *Tell your therapist.*

Hurt once again because you feel gas-lit and blamed for the very same argument? *Tell your therapist.*

Worried you're trapped in an engagement not meant for you? *Tell your therapist.*

Filled with self-loathing and feelings of unworthiness, destined to fall short of what society expects of you? *Tell your therapist.*

Scared by the fact that not one person around you seems to have any clue what is really going on in your life? *Tell your therapist.*

Deeply depressed? *Tell your therapist.*

You get the picture.

And yet, there I was, keeping absolutely all of these very thoughts and doubts to myself for months. I told The Trusty Therapist about arguments or general issues I was having with Mr. Ex for sure, but the deeper knowing at how hopelessly unaligned we were in all the things that really mattered in life? Nope, those stayed well and properly buried within. By covering those truths, glossing over what I was feeling, and photoshopping my reality just enough, I was actually lying to her face. I was lying to the one person who I knew had the capacity to help me decipher my feelings. I was lying to The Trusty Therapist, and thereby myself.

Until suddenly I couldn't lie to either of us anymore.

As I recall, it went a little something like this...

I walked into the waiting room and took my usual seat in the corner of the small antechamber. I sat by the window and peered out at the brilliant spring trees filling the courtyard of the petite French restaurant below. It was usually an oasis of calm in the center of bustling Larimer Square, but on this day, I couldn't shake the nerves and the anxiety that had stalked me down the city blocks. I'm a nervous sweater by nature, so when I felt the perspiration start, I realized just how worried and worked up I was.

A feeling of foreboding came over me as I tried to fortify myself for the performance to come. I was still determined to keep my calm and carry on, but my body was curiously betraying me.

"Well, this is gonna suck," I thought briefly before The Trusty Therapist came to fetch me.

"Come on in, Katherine." She beckoned me forward with a warm smile as she had done hundreds of times before.

I gulped and followed her into the doom, I mean room.

Sitting rigidly on the small, pale gray couch, I clutched a charcoal pillow to my chest like a child clinging to her favorite stuffed animal. I fiddled nervously with my cuticles, one of my surefire tells even now, picking the edges so vigorously they began to bleed a bit.

Damn.

I reached for a Kleenex to disguise my self-injurious behavior while she gathered her papers and came to sit elegantly across from me.

"Where shall we start today?" she asked innocently enough.

I don't remember exactly what prompted my sudden willingness to be completely and totally unfiltered and honest, but my body was obviously ready for the eruption. I physically couldn't keep it all inside any longer, and like a volcano about to explode, the pressure built and built and begged for a release.

Eyes wide with abject terror, the smallest of confessions escaped my lips.

"I'm having doubts."

"Doubts about what?" she asked, looking back at me serenely.

Unable to put the genie back in the bottle, I continued. "About the wedding. I'm having doubts. I'm not sure I can marry Mr. Ex," I all but whispered as I lowered my head in shameful repentance for my confession.

An immediate wave of guilt swept over me like the infamous rogue waves that capsize even the most experienced of seafarers. I thought I would drown in my shame as I sank further into the couch and further into myself, trying with all my might to disappear into oblivion, into nothingness.

I had just divulged the biggest secret of my entire life, and now that it was said aloud, I couldn't take it back. Like the exposed brick walls around us, my painstakingly built façade came crumbling down. I sat there naked and vulnerable and scared, waiting for her response.

But like the lifeline she had always been, The Trusty Therapist wasn't about to let me drown. I don't even think she was particularly surprised. She told me she had sensed what I was feeling even before I was ready to admit it, but ever the teacher, she had allowed me to get to a place of acceptance in my own time. She then gave me a safe space to spill it all, and I did.

I unloaded all the negative emotions, thoughts, and realities I was facing. Everything I had held back from telling my friends and family, save Mr. New Orleans, for the last nine months came spilling out. With The Trusty Therapist I could be totally and completely honest. No holding back. No hiding. Session after session. Truth after ugly truth.

Unsurprisingly, it helped. The initial release was indeed heady and huge, but after that first period of emotional eruption, the hard work began.

I was finally honest, bare, totally unmasked, and ready to explore the meaning of my newly acknowledged truth.

Looking back, the most memorable bit about this entire process was the one question The Trusty Therapist began asking me at the start of every session.

Each week as I marched closer and closer to the altar, she would begin with, "If you had to decide today, what percentage of you would want to get married and what percentage of you would want to walk away?"

Some days I was 90 percent get married, 10 percent walk away.

Others I was 75 percent to 25 percent.

Even worse, there were days of only 5 percent yay and 95 percent nay.

Over time, the levels fluctuated, but the exact number on a given day wasn't really what mattered. What was helpful was how the exercise forced me to think through my own decision-making process and commit to a concrete answer, even if it was temporary.

True, it provided a level of analytical and mathematical detachment, which my brain loved, but that wasn't all. Not only did it open the door to the possibility of an alternate reality for my future, but it let me choose the probability with which that alternate universe would come to fruition. It gave me ownership over my doubts and helped me to weigh them in a meaningful way. By quantifying them, the doubts became less amorphous and overwhelming. Also, the exercise allowed me to talk about them from a conscious, decision-making place in my psyche.

The exercise didn't force me into a choice, because I don't think I ever got to a place of 100% walk away, but it did ask me to make small, hypothetical choices on a daily basis, so I could try that on and live in that alternate reality, even if just for a moment.

To me, this simple question was an absolute game changer, and a tactic I still use to this day.

"If you had to decide today, what percentage of you would want to quit your job and what percentage of you would want to tough it out?"

"If you had to decide today, what percentage of you would want to face the challenges of freezing your eggs and what percentage of you would want to risk never having a family?"

Trust me, the list of applicable situations goes on and on.

I advise you to give it a try yourself the next time you're in a quandary of this sort. It may just be your best mate as well.

Now, back to therapy.

Over time, we dove deeper into the reasons behind my doubts. We also explored the cold hard facts I would have to come to terms with if I ended up walking away from the future I had planned. If I walked away at age thirty-two, I would secure my spot as the resident spinster of my hometown. Was I willing to inhabit said stereotype? We grieved this potential loss.

If I walked away, I may never be blessed with the opportunity to have biological children of my own. Could I be ok with that? We grieved this potential loss.

If I walked away from this wedding, my grandfather might never see me get married. He may never walk me down the aisle. Was I still willing to do it? We also grieved this loss.

We grieved all those potential losses that were forcing me into a fate I did not want, not in preparation to walk away, but as a way to remove them as the deciding factors in my current situation. Talking about each of them in turn and how they made me feel helped me to reframe my thinking and ultimately remove their power over me. We removed the bars, one by one, and sought to destroy the prison I had trapped myself in. Each time we removed one, we gave the power back to my authentic self and allowed her to explore what she knew she wanted and deserved.

Our conversations were equal parts tedious and tough, for both of us. And though I imagine my therapist wanted to scream "DON'T DO IT" several times at the top of her lungs, she never ever did. Without judgment or direction toward a "right" decision, she let me process slowly and carefully and methodically. She gave me the space to explore and the confidence to let my scary thoughts see the light of day, imagining a reality that was very different to the path I was currently on.

A lot of people describe therapy as unpacking, and I completely connect to this visualization.

I'd enter her office, slowly unpack each piece of anxiety, each doubt, desire or need and lay them out before her like a sidewalk salesman displaying my wares. I'd lighten the heavy, heavy load of the baggage I carried around on a daily basis, and sometimes, as I repacked them to leave, I'd find I no longer needed to take a particular item along for the rest of my journey. I'd leave a previously deemed "essential" fear behind and walk out ever so slightly lighter, stronger, and surer.

They were baby steps, but they were still progress.

Chapter 7

Decision Made

"The more you trust your intuition, the more empowered
you become, the stronger you become,
and the happier you become."
— Gisele Bündchen, *Vogue*

Wedding Countdown: Seventeen days to go
In the many years since the events of this book
transpired, I have had countless conversations about one
particular life-altering moment...

The moment it finally "clicked."

The moment I pushed past the denial, embraced my
doubts, and listened to my intuition.

The turning point, the moment of truth, the point of no
return–call it what you will.

It was the moment I made my choice.

No matter who asks, no matter the gender, age, cultural
background, relationship status–hell, even their level of
acquaintance with me–no matter what, without fail, people
always ask me the exact same question...

"How did you know?"

Sure, countless people want to know about the logistics
of calling off a wedding.

How did you tell your guests? What did you do with your dress? What about the honeymoon?

The follow ups go on and on, and I will include all those gory details in chapters to come, but mostly, people genuinely want to hear about the "how" of this precise moment. The "how" I knew I had to call it off.

Maybe they're asking because they've also struggled with their own calling it off moment in life.

Maybe they want to know so they can advise a friend, a sister, aunt, brother, or grandparent for that matter.

Maybe they're asking out of admiration.

For some, I have no doubt it's merely morbid fascination. I mean, if it weren't my story, I would definitely be curious about this particular moment as well.

I'll venture a guess that most of you reading this can relate to the feeling of a slowly building snowball of dread for some unwanted moment in your lives. It may not have been before your wedding, but you've probably had at least one of those panic-inducing scenarios. You know, the moments that, without you knowing it, change the trajectory of your life entirely. The moments of sudden clarity, and the subsequent relief. Some of you can even grasp the shorthand explanation I sometimes offer in this particular situation: "I just knew it wasn't meant for me."

Yet even for those who relate to this feeling, most people still struggle to grasp *how* I was able to summon the courage not only to make such a totally and completely life-changing decision, but possess the sense of self and conviction to follow through with it.

"But *how?*" they all ask.

And so, after years of therapy, personal growth, journaling, and self-reflection, here is my attempt to answer the seemingly simple, yet astoundingly complex question of *how* I was able to make the hardest, albeit best, decision of my life.

* * *

With only two weeks until the wedding, for better, or for worse, I flew back to New York alone this time.

I may not have a lot of data, but in my opinion, May in New York is utterly fantastic. The weather is spectacular as the sun shines down and a cool breeze blows through the city streets. The flowers are stunning with the cherry blossoms in full bloom, and Central Park is absolutely buzzing with energy and events and life. It's vibrant. It's alive. To me, it's joy personified and the perfect time for a Big Apple fix.

Yet, despite my deeply ingrained love of spring in the city, I was uncharacteristically melancholy.

Perhaps worse than melancholy actually–more like muted. I was a gray-scale gal in the midst of a technicolor dream world as Counting Crows' "Colorblind" played in my head. On pause, and almost disconnected altogether, I suppressed all emotion as I navigated my way through the lively boroughs like a walking, talking zombie-bride.

Reality unfolded around me unnoticed, like a TV show playing in the background you forgot to pause, only to look up ten minutes later and realize you've somehow jumped ahead three scenes. One minute I was deplaning. Then before I knew it, I'd blinked back to life and was checking into my hotel.

How did I get here? I wondered with mild concern.

I watched myself nod my gratitude at the kind front desk attendant. Usually, I'm all smiles, and southern charm, and warmth, but my current "thank you" nod didn't even register on the Richter Scale of kindness.

Something was undeniably and indisputably wrong.

I mean, yes, I had indeed embraced my doubts about the wedding, but I was still deeply confused about how on earth I was going to get myself out of this situation. For though I knew in my gut what I needed to do, I hadn't decided to actually do it yet. I'd spent months anguishing over this decision and still, with just two weeks to go, I was paralyzed by indecision.

So, on I trudged.

I taxied downtown to the Amsale bridal studio in SoHo, arriving a very uncharacteristic hour behind schedule. For someone who believes "on time" is ten minutes early, my lack of reaction to this development and glaring lack of grace at the inconvenience I was clearly causing the amazing women of Amsale was shocking. It was as if I had turned down the volume of my emotions so far that barely a whisper of feeling could escape. As if I was not so much acting in the movie of my own life, but rather being pulled through it by invisible puppet strings. The whole effect was jerky and unnatural. I disassociated further still as two beautiful seamstresses dressed my wooden marionette body in my reception dress, twirled me around and revealed their jaw-droppingly gorgeous work.

"It fits nicely" was all I heard myself utter as my jaw moved up and down to the pluck of the universal threads.

No gushing, no smile, definitely no tears of joy. Just a matter of fact "thanks," and I was tapped out on my final fitting with the wedding goddess that is Amsale. I should have showered them with the infinite gratitude I did actually feel for all of the hard work they put into making such a stunning dress. It wasn't their fault I was a disaster.

But I just couldn't. I didn't have the energy, even though I knew how rude my reaction came off. It goes without saying, my meager response was a clear warning sign.

Turning away from the mirror, I asked morosely, "Can I please take it off now?"

They glanced at each other, exchanging a look I can only assume was pity, and swiftly helped me disrobe without so much as a word.

As I was silently stripped–a shockingly recurrent theme throughout the entire wedding dress experience–a thought briefly registered through the numbness in my brain: *I should probably apologize for my confusing behavior.* Yet, as quickly as the notion came, it floated away. I was clearly no longer in control here.

Whether or not the modistes suspected this was the beginning of the end, I can't conclusively say. But, I can guarantee you they were perplexed at best. Come to think of it, they probably knew exactly what I was struggling with. After all, they see bride after bride on the reg, and I bet they are pretty skilled at pinpointing who will make it down the aisle, and in my case, who won't.

Unlike the brides in most happily-ever-after wedding tales, I was but a small step above catatonic. I marched forward mechanically, trying to accomplish my wedding to-do list, even though I felt completely trapped by the very same thing I was planning.

As I taxied back uptown for my final dress fitting at Monique Lhuillier, I thought, *One last stop, and then all the planning will be over. One last scene as the perfect bride, and then I can shut down, reboot, and catch my breath.*

Maybe then, I could figure out what the heck I was going to do.

"One last stop," I uttered, as I hoped out of the cab and walked toward the atelier.

You got this, I thought, as I tried to pep talk my way to the *fin du monde.*

Deep breath in.

Deep breath out.

Shoulders back. Spine straight. Head held high. I tugged on the filaments of my puppeteer and tried to muster as much gusto as possible for the last obstacle of my day. Oversized black sunglasses firmly in place because I've never been able to depuff my eyes after days of crying, no matter how strongly I *gua sha.* Feelings curled tight down into the pit of my stomach.

Muscles tensed in upon themselves so hard it hurt. It was as if I was afraid my very soul would flee my body if I unclenched my vice grip for even one infinitesimal second. Every fiber of my body was screaming to be heard. Screaming for escape.

And still, I fought for control.

Here I go, I thought.

Summoning every last ounce of energy I had left, I swung open the doors with a plastic smile plastered across my gaunt and sunken-eyed visage.

Led by the sales associate, I proceeded upstairs to the dressing rooms, passing slowly by dress after dress, which for some reason felt like an anonymous funeral procession passing by unmarked graves. As I reached the chamber at the end, my own gown hung in the doorway, its lacey train splayed ceremoniously across the floor. My breath caught strangely in my throat, but I discreetly coughed and tried to mask my anxiety.

Carefully, I slipped into my newest costume. Layer upon layer of the most delicate French lace and ivory tulle were ready and waiting to prop me up from the outside in. The fabric held me immobile with its spindly webs of marital mirage, attempting to lock me in as the "good wife" for good. The seamstress fastened the corset around my waist like a rapidly tightening noose, zipping me securely into a future as Mrs. Ex. She trapped my body like I'd already trapped my soul.

It was time.

I emerged from the changing room to a circular room with walls so full of floor-length mirrors the effect of the reflections surrounding me made it look like I was in Versailles. My gaze remained steadfastly cast upon the floor as I prepared to face my reflection. I braced for impact.

Cautiously, I raised my eyes to meet the stare of the figure in the mirror.

And then there I was, unable to hide for a moment more.

Totally stripped.

Dressed to the nines but totally exposed.

Raw.

Real.

Ready.

Waiting.

Deep breath in.

Deep breathe out.

I took a good, hard, honest look. And for the first time in months, I finally saw the woman staring back at me.

I saw her stoic, resolved, practiced reflection, but *she* was not *me*. She was a perfectly coiffed, perfectly dressed, perfectly polished statue. She was voiceless, silently betraying what she truly wanted and accepting her fate with equanimity, grace, and dignity. She was choosing to stay rather than run.

But me?

As for me, I was gone.

This woman cannot be me, I thought.

Her fear, so plainly hiding behind her vacant eyes, it was all mine. But her faux happiness, her Stepford smile— neither were my truth. Her dress, though stunning, was not my dress. Her over-the-top, out-of-control wedding was not authentic to me in any way, shape, or form. Her husband- to-be was not my forever partner. This life, this future staring back at me, this could not be me.

This will not be me!

As the veil lifted, all of my truths were released in a flood of determined realization. I broke free, ripping violently through the surface of my ever-calm pool of the dutiful bride. Gasping for precious air, I declared: *ENOUGH.*

With that, I was pulled forcefully back into my body. Reunited with the newly embodied truth inside, I reinhabited my long-lost self. I was still terrified, yes, but I was somehow calmer and more at peace than I had been in months. I knew what I had to do, and this time, I was not afraid to do it.

Deep breath in.

Deep breathe out.

From the outside, there no dramatic or even perceptible shift. Throughout all the drama in my mind, the utterly endearing dressmaker never even broke her train of thought. Physically, I had not moved an inch. I was still standing on the same riser, in exactly the same dress, looking at the exact same reflection.

And yet, on the inside, the change was seismic. Where there was unending cold before, there was now the faintest whisper of warmth. Where there was trepidation, there was now bravery and confidence. Where there was sorrow, miraculously, there was now hope. The most terrifying and elusive of all emotions.

Hope.

I released the last drop of long-held breath with a sigh so big I felt like even my toes were exhaling.

I finally had hope.

For the remainder of my last dress fitting, I nodded graciously, not wanting to offend anyone in the process. I politely pretended to make mental notes about my trains and bustles and such. I even had the wherewithal to ask for videos of how to properly bustle the dress I now knew I had zero intention of wearing in two weeks' time.

I proffered my sincerest appreciation for the seamstress's spectacular work, paid my remaining balance to the associate out front, confirmed the shipping address, and drifted out the front door back onto E. 71st Street–practically gliding on my cloud of acceptance for what I'd decided to do.

I felt unflappable, some might even say serene, as I meandered across the busy boulevard to Central Park, sat on a bench, and slowly pulled out my phone. Looking down at the lock-screen of engagement-sessions past I briskly swiped it open and dialed my one true person, my best friend, The Ride or Die.

Before she could even get out her usual loud and upbeat greeting, I blurted out, "I'm not getting married."

Obviously stunned, but not deterred, she waited for a beat that felt like an eternity before she asked one very simple question, "Are you sure?"

Not, "Oh my gosh no! You can't do this." Not, "Are you crazy?" Not any of the one million things she could have said that would have shown her shock, or awe, or doubt, or confusion, or–worse–judgment. Just an "Are you sure?" filled with acceptance, support, and love. It was the perfect combination of complex emotions distilled down to three simple words. She nailed it once again.

"Yes," I reiterated with a determined nod of my head.

Always the pragmatist, she continued, "Well, then what's your plan, and how can I help?"

Still unsure of how to answer either of those questions, I replied, "I honestly have no idea what I'm going to do or when I'm going to do it. All I know is I'm completely and totally certain this is the right choice. This is what I want." I repeated out loud what I said inside my head only moments before: "This will not be me."

Looking back, I think this was as much for my own benefit as it was to answer her query.

And with this simple statement of truth, I finally set myself free.

Deep breath in.

Deep breath out.

* * *

Now, I know this whole scene may seem a bit dramatic or unrealistic or even flat out impossible. And if you haven't been through this sort of out-of-body experience, watching yourself act in real time but mentally removed from it all, then it may never make a lick of sense. Even so, I can all but guarantee that some of you, if you're honest with yourself, know exactly the feeling I just described.

The moment where, through an out-of-body experience, *what* to do next is so crystal clear it's both maddening and laughable that it took this long to decide. The moment of confirmation your authentic self has been right all along. The moment that forever alters your life from this day forward. The moment you choose you, first and foremost, forever and ever, 'til death do you part, as long as you both shall live.

I'm not naïve enough to think that at least some of you may be slightly disappointed here. You're looking back, flipping pages, rereading, searching for more salacious answers to the question of *why* Mr. Ex and I weren't right for each other.

Why exactly did I decide Mr. Ex wasn't my life partner? *Why* did we self-destruct in what appears to be a little under a year's time? *Why* weren't we getting married in possibly one of the most beautiful and spectacularly planned wedding celebrations I could possibly imagine?

Well, even though calling it off may seem drastic to you, I can assure you it wasn't. It was the long, slow process of shifting the focus from Mr. Ex and his behavior back to me and mine. Back to what I was willing to tolerate. Back to the future and the marriage I wanted. Even back to the environment I wanted to create for my kids one day. The focus all came back to me.

Despite our efforts to align, Mr. Ex and I did not want the same life.

We did not have the same values and goals.

We didn't agree on what it means to have a healthy dynamic.

We didn't handle conflict in the same way.

There were anger issues, substance issues, and communication issues. Issue after issue after issue. Pretty much whatever issues there were to have in a relationship, we probably had them.

We loved each other deeply, but our issues were insurmountable. After a year of fighting for it, or rather about it, our relationship was truly broken beyond repair. People as ill-matched as we were are never meant to be married, and I think it was a blessing we did not start a life together, let alone a family.

I couldn't imagine raising kids together, and though I did have to come to terms with the fact that calling off this wedding might mean I would never have biological children of my own, I figured no kids was a better outcome than raising them with someone I knew would never be on the same page as I.

In the end, it all came down to this one statement—Mr. Ex was not my person.

Beyond this fact, a more detailed *why* would be focusing on Mr. Ex, instead of me, and those particular details don't stinking matter, y'all.

The very unique facets of our *why* won't help you choose yourself any more than your *why* would have helped me, because it is different for each person and each relationship. My *why* is a piece of my personal story, yes, but to me, the *why* isn't nearly as profound as the universally applicable *what's* and *how's* of this book.

But here's the amazing part: the *what's* and the *how's* are actually the good bits here! They're the golden nuggets of wisdom I managed to glean from this situation. Hell, they're the reason to read this book.

How did you decide to call it off?

What did you do next?

How did you survive burning your life into itty bitty charcoaled bits?

What did it all feel like?

How did you rebuild?

What is life like on the other side of destruction?

And maybe most of all, was calling it off worth it?

What remains the utmost important message here is I knew it. I knew it. I knew it. I knew it. Deep, deep down in my core, in the essence of my being, in the most intuitive recesses of my soul, I knew it. I knew it all along. And what's more, beyond knowing it, I *finally* trusted myself when I decided what I had to do next.

That's the key here.

Not the details of *why* we failed as a couple, but the unquestionable certainty I felt of my *"what* do I do now?"

Deep breath in.

Deep breath out.

KATHERINE ROSE WOLLER

Part II
Let It Burn

Out of the night that covers me,
Black as the Pit from pole to pole,
I thank whatever gods may be
For my unconquerable soul.
In the fell clutch of circumstance
I have not winced nor cried aloud.
Under the bludgeonings of chance
My head is bloody, but unbowed.
Beyond this place of wrath and tears
Looms but the Horror of the shade,
And yet the menace of the years
Finds, and shall find, me unafraid.
It matters not how strait the gate,
How charged with punishments the scroll,
I am the master of my fate:
I am the captain of my soul.
                    – William Ernest Henley, "Invictus"

KATHERINE ROSE WOLLER

Chapter 8

The Hardest Conversation
I've Ever Had

"Everything you've ever wanted
is on the other side of fear."

– George Addair

Wedding Countdown: Sixteen days to go
I awoke the next morning, still bleary-eyed, still exhausted, and still in New York, but still knowing exactly what I had to do.

My metanoia had begun. Our wedding was only two weeks away, and I needed to decisively call off our nuptials now or forever hold my peace.

What's more, not only did I need to call off the event itself, but I also needed to end an almost three-year relationship at the very same time, knowing full well I was going to break Mr. Ex's heart, my own, and potentially the hearts of both of our entire families.

I imagined telling my mom and my grandfather and could all but see the utmost disappointment on their faces. I thought about Mr. Ex's Nanny and Pop and acutely felt their painful reactions. I thought everyone would think I was a failure, and though obviously they didn't, I built it all up in my mind. Funny how we can torture ourselves far more in our minds than reality ever could.

To say I was trepidatious is a gross understatement. But nervous as I was, I was also resolute and unwavering in my knowing. I believed in my truth, and I would no longer be swayed from the path I needed to take.

Even then, the question of how on earth I was going to extricate myself from this cage of my own design remained daunting, and I had no earthly idea what to say to Mr. Ex.

No idea what to do. Nada. Zilch. Zero. A big old goose egg. I was at a complete and total loss, and for the first time in ages, the right words completely escaped me.

I needed time to ruminate, time to formulate a strategy, time to organize my thoughts into cohesive sentiments, because going into such a life-altering conversation without a step-by-step plan seemed almost as impossible as getting married in two weeks time.

Almost.

Thankfully, a literal act of God bought me twenty-four-hours of additional think-time before I had to return home, as a freak thunderstorm the size of the tri-state area descended upon New York. It blanketed the city in a true torrential downpour. Thunder clapped ceremoniously as the winds swept across the Hudson River, creating white caps fit for the sea, and it was like the lights were on a dimmer switch when the black clouds covered the sun, turning day into night. Needless to say, my flight home was delayed.

Sitting at a coffee shop on the lower levels of Newark Airport, I repeatedly checked the radar and prayed for more time to prepare. Refresh, refresh, refresh. Sip, sip, sip. Pray, pray, pray. I tried to process the life-altering decision I had made, but instead I just sat there, swinging my foot in the same nervous habit I've had since I was in grade school, silently kicking under the desk to self-soothe. Waiting, just waiting to find out when I would return home. Hoping the storm would bring momentary relief and letting out a proper sigh of relief when I finally received a notification that my flight now had a full seventeen-hour delay until the following morning.

Thank. The. Lord.

With limited options and a very early morning flight, I decided to stay at the closest possible option to the airport. Once checked in at the Embassy Suites Newark Airport, I flopped on the bed without even pulling back the comforter and clicked on the TV to kill some of the upcoming seventeen hours without so much as a hairbrush. There was no luggage to unpack, since my suitcases were still firmly ensconced in the bowels of a 747 somewhere, and though the emotional baggage of the trip could definitely have used some sorting, it was too heavy to lift at the moment.

Laying on the bed crying and trying to sort out what in the world I was supposed to say to Mr. Ex the next day, I was immediately sucked into a *Beat Bobby Flay* marathon on Food Network, my favorite since I was a little kid staying up late to watch the original *Iron Chef*, subtitles and all. Why I still remember this particular detail, I'm not sure. But I do remember I found the foodie-fluff comforting, like perfectly made cheese grits with salt and pepper, or piping hot macaroni and cheese, or my all-time favorite, "biscuits debris," from my hometown diner, Jimmy's Egg, which is basically glorified biscuits and sausage gravy with cheddar cheese and even more sausage on top.

You see, I LOVE to cook, as it calms my golden retriever-esque brain, and thankfully, watching the expert chefs slice, dice, and confidently create organization and beauty out of chaos was even better comfort food than the actual comfort food of my childhood.

A few episodes passed, and the tears began to subside.

So despite the unfamiliar bed, despite the thundering storm outside and the turmoil within, I miraculously and peacefully slept.

* * *

Wedding Countdown: Fifteen days to go

With my New Jersey delay complete, it was finally time to pay the piper, only this time there was no hope of a freak natural disaster to buy me any more time.

Back at the airport, I ached for clean clothes to wear for the sorrowful journey home, so I bought a super soft navy and white NY Yankees hoodie and layered it under my hot pink, tweed trench. Sort of an unexpectedly cool look, actually, but mostly I was just glad it wasn't covered in snot and tear stains.

I flew the four hours back to Denver in a dreamy, far-off daze, assuming I would be able to get home, settle in, and collect my thoughts while Mr. Ex was still at work. I planned to spend the few hours before he arrived home showering, gathering my strength, and, most importantly, crafting the perfect soliloquy to deliver at a well-timed break in our upcoming conversation.

I had to be kind, but firm. I had to be true to me, but still compassionate to the heart I was well aware I was about to break. I had to be composed, succinct, and ideally confident in my delivery. Perhaps it could be so beautifully spoken it would make the situation go smoothly? Maybe it could even ease both our pain and deliver us peacefully to the other side of a breakup? Could it protect us both from further hurt? Probably not, but maybe it could set us both free.

Once again, the universe had other plans.

I parked my mid-size SUV, which I foolishly bought a few months earlier because it was a sensible mom car and I mistakenly assumed I would be "Mom" in no time, and crossed our small backyard to the patio door, sighing with relief as I prepared to turn the handle and enter my home, my safe space.

Cue shock and awe.

Not only was Mr. Ex home instead of at work where he was supposed to be, he was also in the kitchen, and having heard me pull up, opened the back door right as I reached for the knob.

My eyes must have bulged out of my head like an old school Wiley Coyote cartoon before I was able to regain my composure and utter a surprised, "Oh, hello," but Mr. Ex. didn't seem to notice said eye-bulge.

I wheeled my bags into the kitchen and parked them next to the big, white, marble island that dominated the open concept kitchen/dining/living room space of my bungalow. An orange tea kettle sat beautifully on the modern gas stove as meticulously placed rose chintz dishes and vintage, green depression glasses glistened from the open shelves. Every single bit of modern and antique domestic bliss in its place. Every item where it should be. Every piece of the veneer secure, not knowing it was all about to be shattered into a million tiny bits.

Fearing my knees would give out from the sudden adrenaline rush, I perched stiffly on the nearest brushed-steel bar stool and swiveled to face Mr. Ex as he stood across from me on the other side of the island. I had the brief thought he might as well have been an ocean away, rather than only an island, but I was quickly snapped back as he started in with a shockingly normal conversation. I tried to regain my equilibrium, running through various exit scenarios in my head and only half listening to the words coming out of his mouth. Then I heard it: Mr. Ex was talking about wedding gifts.

He said he wanted to get me something I would really love and stated he was considering pearl earrings.

Pearl earrings?!? I cried inside my head.

I mean, YES, pearls would be right up my alley and normally I would be overwhelmed by such a thoughtful gift, but NO, there was no way I could let him buy something so expensive when I knew the wedding was never going to happen. Absolutely not. No way in hell. No way around it.

It's time, I thought resolutely.

You could say it was the pearl that broke the camel's back, for I could not in good conscience keep going for even one second longer.

Without thinking, I ordered the firing squad to commence, no well-rehearsed monologue in sight.

"Wait," I whispered.

"What do you mean wait? Is it the earrings? Do you not want pearls?" he asked. "I can think of other ideas if you want something else."

"It's not the pearls. I don't want any gift at all. I don't want you to buy me anything."

Fear slowly crept into his response as some part of his brain knew the long-awaited eventuality that was about to come to fruition, "Why don't you want me to buy you anything?" His body language changed and whereas a moment before he was relaxed and even excited by the perfect gift he had landed upon, he was now on high alert, like he himself was ready to attack.

Finally confronted with the moment, I braced for impact.

And with a deep breath in, I said, "I don't want you to buy anything because I do not want to marry you."

The words hung in the air with the anticipatory moment of silence between when you see the lightning and when you finally hear the thunderous crack. Still holding my breath, I waited for the crash. I had said it. I had finally spoken my truth. Now, it was time to face the boom.

With the intensity and rapidity of a southern summer thunderstorm, the skies suddenly ripped open, and the torrents unleashed. A deluge of screaming, yelling, tears, threats, pleading, confusion, insults, and hurt swirled around our kitchen. My head spun as I struggled to determine which way was up. It was a rush of emotion with such force it actually stole the air from the room.

I couldn't breathe.

And still, we battled on.

Two lovers, locked in a savage war.

It still hurts me to remember it.

Mr. Ex pulled out all the stops to convince me I had made the wrong choice. He even pulled out his phone and called his mother on speakerphone to both tell her the news and torture me simultaneously. "Katherine just called off the wedding," he said, no segues, no qualifiers, and then he hung up as his mom was still mid-sentence asking, "What's going on?!?" He was trying to manipulate me back into changing my mind, knowing the shame his sudden act of calling his mother, who I loved and respected, would bring inside me. Only it backfired. For the first time, his well-practiced tactics didn't bring me back in line; rather, they strengthened my resolve and allowed me to calm myself and forge ahead.

It felt like hours upon hours of brutal back and forth.

To put it bluntly, it was hell, and remains the single most difficult, heartbreaking, and world-altering conversation I've ever had.

And yet, despite the fire burning me from the inside out, I fought to go cold, fought to withstand the heat. I forced myself to calm, going numb and wrapping detachment around me like a superhero's cape. I was holding onto my composure for dear life, hoping the fire would burn itself out before I perished in its blaze entirely. I could not allow myself to be consumed by the energy, for if I relented for even one moment, I might allow myself to be drawn back into the grasp of my would-be future.

I could not give in.

No matter how harsh or hurtful my cold detachment made me in the moments that followed, it was the only way I could withstand the inferno. I had to choose myself, my future, my truth.

Be strong, Katherine, be strong. Stand your ground.

Finally, after what seemed like an eternity spent at Dante's mercy, the heat subsided, and Mr. Ex stormed off. Slamming the door behind him, he peeled out of our driveway in his big black truck and headed speedily to parts unknown. As swiftly as it started, it stopped.

There was quiet.

So, so, so much quiet.

In the blissful void, I shuddered a sigh of relief and officially dropped the weight of the world to my original hardwood floors.

"*It is done,*" whispered my authentic self reassuringly. "*You are free.*"

* * *

It was official, there was no more "us."

There was no more wedding.

I was no longer a bride-to-be.

In nothing more than a few short hours, *we* were no longer a "we."

I wanted to collapse with relief, but I was equal parts exhilarated and terrified, and I needed to get the heck out of the house, and fast, lest Mr. Ex decided to return and gear up for round two.

I needed space and time alone to process the events of the last few hours, and Mr. Ex deserved the same. So, I sent a quick and admittedly not super informative text to my own mom, vaguely letting her know the wedding was off. Then, true to form, I fled up the road to The Ride or Die's house around the corner.

I walked into her North Denver bungalow and all I wanted was to cocoon myself in a blanket, collapse into a ball, and finally fall completely and totally to pieces. I had held it together for so long, I could feel I was about to come unglued. Unfortunately, when I walked in, I remembered she truly had all of zero comfortable furniture in her entire house. No cushy couches, no well-worn reading chair, not even a bean bag. Nada.

Not one to be deterred from a meltdown, we went to her room, and I immediately crumpled to the shag-carpet-covered floor. It was soft and completely and totally solid. In some ways, it was the perfect place to surrender, for what could possibly be more grounding than the ground itself? Plus, I'm a floor sitter by nature and love the feeling of stretching my legs out on the land, reaching through every inch of my being, and clenching all my muscles for just an instant before I release and give my weight to earth. Maybe it's the years of a semi-consistent yoga practice, but feeling the terra firma underneath my body is the default place where I feel most supported. It's my sanctuary.

As it turns out, her beige shag rug was exactly what my aching body and battered heart needed.

That, and The Ride Or Die's big toe resting ever-so-lightly on my pant leg. She is a well-known anti-hugger, and come to think of it, not even really a "toucher" at all, so even though it was technically a minuscule moment of shared bodily surface area, her big toe grazing my leg was a special moment in and of itself. It was her way of hugging me tight, giving me comfort and strength. Her way of wrapping her arms around me and whispering, "Everything will be ok."

I don't know if The Ride or Die will ever know how much that night meant to me, but I will forever be grateful to her for giving me the grace and support I had always craved but feared I might lose when I called it off.

Perhaps you have to know her to understand, but I believed her and her big toe. True, my life was now a total mess. But her big toe was right. With time, everything would be even better than ok.

In this moment, my upended life and unknown future transformed just a smidge from terrifying to the biggest blessing of all. I was suddenly aware of the fact that I was now free to make my life exactly what I wanted.

My inner-self rejoiced.

Upon reflection, I've realized one of the biggest things holding me back from consciously acknowledging my doubts for so long was fear. Fear of judgment. Fear of the gossip mill. Fear of missing out on the blessing of becoming a mother. Fear of what my family would say. Fear of all the external factors at play in any complex and admittedly unhealthy relationship.

I was absolutely terrified of how people would react if I followed through with what my heart knew more and more assuredly as the months wore on post-engagement. What's more, I think fear is what made me betray myself and my truth for so long. The fear held me hostage for eleven months and prevented me from admitting what some part of me knew was true from the moment I said yes to Mr. Ex.

I was also humiliated at the thought of what people back home would say. We all know how quickly word gets around in certain social circles, especially in small towns.

I was sure the verdict would be an all-around unflattering review of my life's choices now that I was once again single and without the main thing that brought me worth in southern society: a man.

I was convinced I would bring shame and disgrace upon my family as a whole. I didn't, but still, my fear knew exactly what to say to keep me walking the line.

Then there was the issue of what my mother would say.

She who had spent hours upon hours and sleepless nights helping to plan this wedding. She who would now have to rapidly help me unplan the same event. She who had believed the façade of my happy life all along and knew nothing about how I was really feeling, save for one tearful conversation in the park. She who would be as blindsided as Mr. Ex. She who generously spared no expense to create the perfect celebration. She sunk fear into my heart.

Not only was I ashamed by the amount of money we had already invested into this endeavor, but I was also genuinely devastated I would be wasting it on a failure.

I felt like I was literally flushing funds down the toilet, and that guilt was crippling. Though it's hard and perhaps unflattering to admit, I was also terrified my mother might make the undeniably sensible decision to refuse to pay for any future wedding to the as-yet-unmet man of my dreams. I'm embarrassed even now to share this, but I felt like this was my only shot at a beautiful wedding, even if it wasn't what or to whom I wanted.

I was petrified to face the shame of it all. Public shame and judgment for which I wasn't positive I was strong enough to face. I felt like I would be the town's new Hester Prynne, Nathaniel Hawthorne's outcast heroine, walking around with a scarlet letter "F" on my chest. Failure, Former Fiancée, Fraud. Take your pick. If the "F" fits, they'll make you wear it.

Add in abject terror and you get the picture.

Each one of these fears was a small but sturdy push in the seemingly unstoppable momentum propelling me toward the altar. They were each a single, sturdy, steel bar in the cage of my own making, and they were the anchors holding me in place.

And yet, I did ultimately manage to conquer these fears. I realized the fear of external judgment was nothing compared to the life I would forever face if I didn't own what my heart wanted. Choosing myself. Prioritizing me. When I looked at my fears from a place of ownership, suddenly they didn't hold as much power. They didn't have as much weight, as much irresistible force. Sure, I was still worried sick about the money and the lack of partnership. Sure, I knew people would talk, and many did. Sure, I was afraid I would lose all of my familial support and friendships in the process, but it was all a small price to pay for my freedom, for my future, for myself.

In the end, I couldn't, I wouldn't put a single one of those factors above my own happiness. I could not let the fear win. I had to prioritize my truth, what my intuition knew to be true. I was certain my marriage to Mr. Ex was not meant to be, and I had to follow my gut.

Blessedly, I was eventually able to overpower my fear. Embracing my authentic knowing empowered me to throw off the shackles of shame and expectation for long enough to confidently face all of the consequences I feared.

Spoiler alert: the people who loved me, my family and friends, did not judge me for a single damn second. They granted me unconditional grace and never-ending support. Hell, some were proud of me. They not only respected my choice, they also loved me without condition, and for that, I am forever in their debt.

But just so you know, if they *had* dropped me like a bad habit, it still would have been worth it.

I would have been worth it.

Years later, I read *Untamed* by Glennon Doyle, and in her book she wrote that in order to build the life and the self you want–who you were put on this planet to be–"we must be willing to let the old burn."

Well, Glennon, I burned.

I burned it all to the freakin' ground.

Chapter 9

The Aftermath

"Hope…which whispered from Pandora's box only after
all the other plagues and sorrows had escaped,
is the best and last of all things."
— Ian Caldwell, *The Rule of Four*

Wedding Countdown: Fourteen days to go
Once my impending marriage had well and truly crumbled around me like pieces of my scrumptious, never-to-be-eaten wedding cake, home was the last place I wanted to be. I dreaded walking in the front door of the house I owned, and the idea of escaping, even just a few miles away, sounded pretty darn amazing. The urge to run is strong with this one, and my guess is a little escapism hits all runaway brides at about this point.

As you can probably guess, this is exactly what I did.

I scampered off down the road and promptly checked into my own personal version of a failed bride, failed wedding, failed woman, failed life, failed everything-I-thought-mattered rehabilitation facility on the tenth floor of a downtown Denver hotel.

Now, I recognize, for a variety of reasons, a lot of people cannot instantaneously check into a hotel down the road. But the point isn't that I craved a hotel. It's that I craved space. It could have been a friend's house, my mom's, a sister's. I just needed a place of my own. A place to be alone. I needed a safe harbor. A place where my raw-as-hell nerves could relax a bit without the threat of a sudden and unseen and wholly undesired jolt of pain around every corner. I needed a respite from my totally devastated, formerly perfect-seeming world where I could hide away, lick my wounds, and heal.

Plus, I was about to attempt to take the inevitable next step of letting the whole world know my decision, and the thought of dealing with anyone, let alone Mr. Ex, while I did it was more than my fragile psyche could bear. I needed a sanctuary to reflect on my decision, which, even though it was my choice, shattered my heart into a million miniscule pieces that I was unsure could ever be knit back together again.

I was drowning in uncertainty and more doubt. This time, however, the doubt was self-doubt, wondering if I had done the right thing. These double trouble twins brought with them a swarm of immediate second-guessing that plagued me like midges in the Scottish summer–encircling and attacking every inch of exposed skin to leave pinprick bites that itch and, when scratched, festers, leaving small but very distinct red scars of pale, newly healed skin. Each one was a reminder of the thoughts running amok in my head.

Why did I just blow up my life?

What the hell was I thinking?

Dear God, what do I do now?

Over and over and over, like an out of control Ferris wheel I couldn't get off. A runaway train of over analyzing, doubt, and fear–my same old fear, just with a new refrain–crept into every thought.

That, right there. The unknowing, the fear. *That* was the worst. It was my final obstacle to overcome.

In the space between privately calling it off and publicly announcing my choice, fear was my foremost enemy, and if I wasn't careful, fear would drag me back into my cage once more. Fear would snatch my hard-fought freedom before I internalized the love and hope it would one day bring.

Whereas twenty-four hours before I knew exactly what my future held, I now had less than zero clues as to what my life was going to be like five years from now, six months from now, hell, six minutes from now. This was a petrifying thought in and of itself. Even though I had dreaded the future I saw before me, at least I saw the dang thing! At least, I was certain what would happen next.

The next week would bring final preparations for the wedding. The week after would be the wedding itself where my grandfather and mother would jointly walk me down the aisle to my future husband. A few months after, we would begin trying for kiddos, dutifully ignoring the unhealthy unhappiness lurking underneath the newlywed veneer. And then a few years down the line, we would live a well-curated, white-picketed fence life that looked perfect on Instagram, despite the reality of what I knew this particular life path would bring.

I knew what I was getting into: I had it all planned out.

Now, peering even one day into my future, I saw nothing but a dark, silent, unknown, unplanned void. Literally nothing. I couldn't even imagine my own story anymore. Not even one day, not to mention a lifetime.

Whenever my mind would wander to this precipice of "what now," intrusive thoughts would dig their nails in, pull me down, and send me spiraling into a vortex of anxiety, dread, and self-loathing. It's what fear of the unknown does to me in even the best of times, and this was so obviously not the best of times.

And yet, spiraling and all, I managed to cling to the one thought that could pull me back from the brink of total oblivion and despair, like it was the last thread of my rapidly fraying lifeline. One thought that brought enough warmth and light to my weary mind so I could lift the cloud of dread long enough to take the next step. One whisper from a previously forgotten and long-ignored friend that proved to be the key to my self-salvation.

Hope.

My wavering certainty at walking away from the life I did *NOT* want was not immediately replaced by knowing the exact details of the life I *DID* want, but it did open the door for possibility.

Blessed possibilities.

It brought the slightest optimism that I could now build the authentic, love-filled, meaningful life I desired and deserved in equal measure. You better believe I clung to this promise with all my might.

Call it faith. Call it intuitive knowing. Call it the Holy Spirit. Call it the universe. Call it what you want. Just call it a blessing. This hope, once embraced, helped me repel the doubtful and dreadful midges in my mind, blocking enough of the fear so I could confidently stay the undeniably rocky course ahead.

Fortunately, my mind took this first moment of liberating hope to spark what would quickly become a lingering obsession for years to come. The idea that would excite and save and heal me on my journey forward: This book!

Only two days out from prioritizing my authentic self over all others and there it was–my flash of inspiration to write and share the entirety of this taboo and unspeakable experience so others do not have to walk this path alone. My tender, glorious, powerful muse. My purpose.

In her book, *Big Magic: Creative Living Beyond Fear*, Elizabeth Gilbert explores this moment by saying the following:

> *The hairs on the back of my neck stood up for an instant, and I felt a little sick, a little dizzy. I felt like I was falling in love, or had just heard alarming news, or was looking over a precipice at something beautiful and mesmerizing, but dangerous…Such an intense emotional and psychological reaction doesn't strike me often, but it happens enough…that I believe I can confidently call it by its name: inspiration.*

Experts try endlessly to understand this most intimate aspect of creating, of art, of inspiration, and almost always fall short with their analysis. However, her words describe precisely how I felt. There are perhaps examples from your own life, your own feelings, where you can relate to this mysticism as well. Now, I'm not a painter, not really anyways. I'm not a sculptor. I'm not even a dancer, though it doesn't stop me from trying. I am a writer. I AM a writer. I am a WRITER.

I ran from this secret passion for so, so, so very long and then, suddenly, here she was, demanding to be heard.

She saw the void in my heart, she saw the real me break free, and finally, she knew it was her opportunity to emerge.

She whispered gently to me like a lover's caress, and for the first time in a long time, I whispered back.

I peeled myself off of the tear-stained sheets of my rented cave and walked the few yards to the classic hotel desk at the far side of the room. I dramatically threw open the black-out curtains and let the Colorado sunlight stream in once again, warming me immediately with its radiant glow. Pausing briefly, I smiled imperceptibly at the cascading heat. I gently eased into the high-backed desk chair, closed my eyes, and rolled my neck slowly from side to side, cracking it gently like the creaks in old floorboards. I opened my eyes to the beautiful June day and grinned weakly as I opened my laptop, my old friend.

Opening a new document, titled simply, "First Draft," I released my guards and let my fingers fly across the keyboard as if they had a mind of their own.

I wrote.

I wrote for hours.

Not well, mind you. Not beautifully, but truthfully and with vigor. I began to transcribe a raw and unedited, some might even call it feverish, account of the events that had transpired, the events to come, the thoughts, the fears, the hope, the despair, the tears, the joy, the freedom, all of it.

I was obsessed. Possessed in my newfound purpose.

In the following days, I scribbled thoughts and run-on sentences in the Notes app of my iPhone. I made voice recordings as I drove to and from the banal errands of my new life. I wrote tipsy deep dives at my local watering holes where a glass of champagne and my laptop led to endless pages of musings I read now with shock and a bit of horror at the bare emotional truths I was willing to share in such a state. I wrote it all, relying on my muse to bring me strength and hope once more.

Let me reiterate, good writing it was *not*. But it was truth, and it was processing in a way only writing can bring for me. The reality is writing saved me. These small acts of recollecting via the written word, slowly but incontestably, brought me back to life. They gave me back my hope.

Even now, I remember the feeling. I wasn't excited per se, because I wasn't looking forward to anything in particular, but I was ecstatic. The intensity of my feeling became overwhelming as I eventually found joy in living life once more. It was euphoric even. Newly single, devastatingly unstable, and yet rapturous with inspiration.

Possessed with a purpose.

Obsessed with creating.

This was truly the first day of the rest of my life.

This was my future.

This was my why.

And this why would miraculously sustain me throughout the trials and tribulations still to come...

Chapter 10

The Formal Uninviting

"The truth will set you free,
but first it will make you miserable."

– James A. Garfield

Wedding Countdown: Thirteen days to go
The deed was done, and now the "fun" had begun. You might think, once I called off the wedding, there really wasn't much more to it. But oh no, my friends. There was so much more to be done. Time to alert the media. Pardon— I mean, alert the guests. More accurately, time to face the oh-so-embarrassing music.

Determining when and how to tell my would-be guests that all was now, in fact, for naught was an intimidating obstacle. Actually, that's putting it mildly. In truth, I was petrified. And on top of abject terror, I was also ashamed. I was confused. I was depressed. I wanted nothing more than to hide away from the world and pretend none of this had ever happened. I wanted to run as far as my little (okay, long) legs would carry me, and yet given that we were only two very short weeks away from the Big Day, I was essentially obligated to inform people immediately. As in I should have told them weeks ago.

It was one thing for me to lose my own money on my failure as a bride-to-be. It was quite another to saddle my friends and family with unused flights to Colorado, lost hotel fees, unnecessary childcare expenses, superfluous black-tie wardrobe items, rental cars, and countless other now useless purchases.

Lacking an alternative escape plan, I surrendered to my fate and got to work.

Even in this once-in-a-lifetime challenge I never in a million years expected to face, I was thankfully able to put my deep-seated control issues and planning obsession to good use. My fragile psyche needed to handle the logistics in a detached yet familiar-to-me kind of way so my brain could achieve some semblance of functionality. I guess it isn't so puzzling then that for some reason I wanted–nay, needed–to handle the uninviting myself.

Perhaps it was self-flagellation for the pain I was causing Mr. Ex.

Perhaps it was attention-seeking.

Perhaps it was pure logic. It seemed fair that if I was the one who called it off, then I, too, should be the one to try to explain the unexplainable.

Perhaps I was just desperate to feel. With every synapse of my brain numbed into submission, maybe the pain of these conversations would allow me to feel something again, anything?

Looking back, though, I think I was craving control over whatever I possibly could.

For so desperately long, I'd felt overwhelmingly out of control of my life. I was strapped into a painful but pretty car on a runaway roller coaster, and I couldn't pull the emergency brake. I knew I was careening toward a future of dread and despair, and yet I felt powerless to change my course. A life out of control. A future commanded by others. The complete and total opposite of self-determination.

Then miraculously, here I was. I pulled the brake. I hit eject and violently ripped myself from that life, forcibly taking my power back. I'd regained my right to rule myself and I'd be damned if I was about to give an ounce of control back to anyone so soon. I wanted to own every last bit of my decision, and I wanted to be the only one who determined my path forward.

From this point on, I was the queen of my own kingdom, however much in shambles it may be. It was my story, my truth, and I was going to be the bard to tell it.

So, marathon to-do lists, efficient and color-coded spreadsheets, and delegation it was. Did I mention I genuinely adore the sight of a color-coded Excel? It's sad, but true.

Thus, step one was to create a way to track who was contacted, by whom and when. For productivity's sake, I duplicated the Excel of our final guest list to create an equally as beautiful but far more morbid version of said list, bluntly named "Cancellation.xls."

Ooof. I cringe even now.

Nevertheless, a quick copy and paste and it was time to get to this depressing work.

The main tab was for *ALL Tracking*. I can tell now I was not exactly thinking straight as this is a horribly nondescript and very unlike me way to name a tab. A tab for *Mom to Contact*. A tab for *Mr. Ex to Contact*. White means they're in the dark. Blue means they know. Notes to record where others graciously agreed to do the deed on my behalf. *Uncle to Call. The Ride or Die to Call. Bridesmaid X to Call. College Roommate Y to Call.* The list went on.

Daunting.

My loved ones deserved to hear the news from me directly, so one by one, I picked up my phone, opened their contact information and forced myself to hit call. It usually went something like this:

Them: Hey there!

Me: I hope I'm not interrupting. Do you have a moment to chat?

Them: Of course! *Still not picking up on the tone of the call.*

Me: Well, *gulp,* I don't want to drag this out, but Mr. Ex and I have decided not to get married and we will be going our separate ways.

Them: Umm. *Silence and shock and awe all rolled into one.* Are you OK?

Me: Not really, but I will be.

Them: Is there anything I can do?

Me: Not now, but maybe later. Thank you for offering. Listen, not to cut this short, but I have a lot of other people to call today.

Them: Oh, sure, sure. Yeah. I guess just call me when you want to talk.

Me: Of course. Will do.

Them: I'll be thinking of you.

Me: Thank you so much. Bye.

I'd hang up the phone and exhale the long-held breath it took to prevent me from giving in to the anguish and tears surging within. An unsteady exhale. A quick scan of the room, and the pull of fresh breath deep into my lungs. Then, an almost imperceptible and surprising lift. A millimeter of lightness as the weight of other people's expectations began to slip from my shoulders. A relaxing of my perpetually clenched jaw.

Huh. Imagine that.

On to the next.

Breathe. Call. Cry. Exhale. Lift.

And so it went.

ON AND ON AND ON AGAIN.

Eventually, my endurance failed me, and with time being of the essence, I resorted to texting those who remained. Too drained and exhausted to care that a text is pretty much the opposite of a thoughtful update. Too fatigued to worry about how rude it was to inform someone of a canceled wedding via text. Too drained to give any more of myself to others. Desperate to complete my distressing to do list, desperate to be bloody well done already, I texted my way to freedom.

Even friends of twenty-plus years got the half-hearted text you read at the outset of this book.

It felt like hundreds, nope thousands, of calls and messages, but it was really only sixty-one folks. Hours agonizing over what I was going to do and fretting about what people would think, and in the end, I only really had to endure sixty-one awkward phone conversations and stilted texts to get to the other side. Sixty-one chats. Sixty-one admissions. Sixty-one iterations of "I'm so sorry."

As expected, Mom swiftly completed her tab as well.

Mr. Ex dutifully completed his tabs, too, and he truly deserves an Olympic medal for this feat. To his credit, he never complained, never argued. He didn't take the golden opportunity to point out the obvious callousness with which I forced myself to handle the situation. Uncharacteristically calm once more, he didn't add fuel to the inferno. Instead, he showed up for me and delivered results. Despite our heartache and combustible states, he selflessly helped me inform our closest friends and family. It was his final gift to me–my wedding gift, I guess you could say.

Words cannot express how thankful I am for this small victory we accomplished together. We were finally supportive partners, even if it was only collaborating on how to end our relationship once and for all. I'd say it was poetic, if it hadn't been so heartbreaking.

In just under twelve hours, we successfully uninvited everyone.

June 2, 2019, 7:49 a.m. MST: It was done.

My computer recorded the exact time I stopped. The exact time I was freed. From that moment on, I literally never opened the file again. That is, until the day I first wrote this chapter. How strange to look back at this collection of names, auto-formatted cells, records of accommodation details, arrival days, allergies, dietary restrictions, etc. The list was nothing more than pixels, and still my emotions went haywire.

A rush of feeling.

Despair.

Elation.

Self-doubt.

Gratitude.

Anxiety.

Desperation.

And above all, hope.

There she was again. Like a swirling soup of contradictions, the mental sensations rose and then fell, quickening my heart and transporting me back to that fateful day. It was like a time machine to my past, unwanted, but oh so effective.

Suddenly, I'm back in my hotel room, huddled like an abandoned and malnourished dog in the small, brown lounge chair in the corner. The scratchy fabric rubbing my skin raw, but I refuse to move from this post. Computer on my lap, iPhone in hand, I glance over at the glass-top desk in the corner where my half-eaten bison burger sits grotesquely, the fat congealed, condensation collecting on the once-melted cheddar slice. Untouched fries still fragrant in the air, despite the fact that they've been sitting there overnight. It's sickening. I gag, but I'm too tired to move the heavy metal tray to the hall. Too forlorn to call the front desk and be forced to deal with another human being.

It's as if I'm watching an old home movie, blurred at the edges, skips and starts, but somehow also vivid and precise, perfectly capturing the emotional sorrow of it all. I doubt I will ever forget those moments. The deep despair threatening to drown me, followed by the totally and completely unmitigated relief.

If you've never had to disappoint all of your closest humans, then you'll just have to take my word for it–it's Dante's ninth circle of hell reserved for the traitor I felt I was. Or perhaps it was the eighth circle, reserved for frauds.

Either way, it was hell.

To write to all the people you love and who love you and inform them, "Surprise! I'm not getting married after all!" To admit you essentially fooled them into believing the fairytale for the last year. To face the fact that you lied to them, for lack of a better word. To experience it all was pure, fiery torture.

Yet, at the same time, I believe it was also an undeniably necessary part of the process for me. Facing these folks helped me to move forward. To feel the weights lift, to notice the rush of relief. Facing my fears and coming out of the darkness feeling invigorated was concrete reassurance once again, I made the right decision.

It also gave me the opportunity to finally accept comfort and counsel from loved ones who had been in this exact situation before, albeit unbeknownst to me. It was during this marathon of uninviting that I learned how many of my closest confidants had been through similar experiences.

Whether they had called off an engagement, or really, really, really wanted to but didn't. Whether they were still married, or now divorced, so many of the women, and men for that matter, in my life were brothers and sisters in this surreal experience. They not only knew my pain, but they knew firsthand the strength it took to call off a wedding. And amazingly, they were nothing but proud of the choice I made. They genuinely opened their hearts to me and consequently showed up for me in ways I never knew were possible. And to this day, I believe we now all talk more openly and truthfully about not just this issue, but all the challenging aspects of life. For this life-altering event in my own story also irrevocably and positively altered my relationships with others.

It allowed me to show my people the real me, flaws and all, and miraculously, they loved me all the more for it.

* * *

There was one more person I had to tell, and though it wasn't technically an uninviting, it felt equally as big.

Whatever her reaction, she was one of the foremost people I NEEDED to share my news with.

It was time to come clean with The Trusty Therapist.

For my first session A.D. (After the Death of my wedding), I was brain-pulsingly hungover. It wasn't my finest moment, and it was not how I wanted to face my beloved therapist, but I couldn't very well skip my session. I had to tell her what had transpired and get to work putting my life and my psyche back together. I needed her help, hangover or no hangover.

I'm still not sure why I was ashamed to tell her. I was relieved with my decision and proud I had chosen myself above all, but I think I still clung to the idea of needing acceptance and support from those I loved, The Trusty Therapist included. I desperately hoped she would still be proud of me, still like me, still keep me as a client. Can you tell I was spiraling a bit?

Sunglasses on to block the blare of the incessant Colorado sun, I rolled up to her office, sat down and ripped off the Band-Aid.

"We're not getting married," I blurted out before she even had the chance to sit down with her pad and pen.

"What?! Wait, slow down. What happened?" She asked, eyes wide with what can only be described as complete shock.

She settled herself in her chair, and I launched into the tale of the whole debacle, including the three tequila and tear-soaked days I'd spent since then.

Apparently not finished with my tears, a deluge poured forth from my eyes as I sobbed the ENTIRE session. It was all I could manage. My nerves were raw from the disaster of my life, and I couldn't hold it together any longer. I had made it through several conversations with Mr. Ex, a night with The Ride or Die, and phone calls galore to would-have-been guests, but I had nothing left to hold me together for this.

And yet, she did not judge me for one. Single. Minute. She didn't think less of me. She was proud. She didn't force me to talk if I couldn't. She waited patiently, content to sit in silence if needed. She didn't leave me broken. And slowly, oh so slowly, when I was finally ready to wield them, she gave me the tools I'd need to rebuild myself, piece by broken piece.

Belief in myself.

Patience.

Compassion.

Gratitude.

Grace.

Love.

One by one, she helped me reclaim the tools of a successful spirit, so I could once again be the warrior goddess, main-character energy, leading lady of my own life.

Ultimately, she empowered me to do what *I* wanted, what *I* needed to do, what *I* felt was right for *me* and *my* future, and then she supported me unconditionally in the aftermath.

It's not an exaggeration to say that she quite literally helped me save myself.

* * *

Now my control-freak story just wouldn't be complete if I didn't at least show you how the final wedding farewell went down.

Given the black-tie formality of our over-two-hundred-person wedding, and the fact that I am a generally traditional person by nature, we decided to send a formal *un*-invitation. It sounds crazy I know, but I felt it appropriate to send a proper written note, especially after my haphazard texting fiasco. Emily Post would be so proud.

Once again, Mr. Ex hated the idea. I mean, rightfully so. He didn't want to call off the wedding in the first place, and therefore felt it was disingenuous to send a joint statement of love and well wishes as a final farewell to our guests. It took some convincing and finagling, but in the end, he signed off on the content and away went the closing arguments to the wedding that wasn't–via first class mail, of course.

In an odd way, I am actually proud of the way we handled this particular piece.

Not to toot my own horn, but the formal un-invitation was *perfection*.

Somber yet elegant pale gray stationary. Thick enough to feel good in the hand, not flimsy, certainly not cheap. Deep charcoal serif text in all caps with proper script signatures. Some simple design flourishes around the border, but nothing overly flamboyant.

Digestible, straightforward messaging. A respectful tone and heartfelt sentiments. A totally true statement of love for each other, at least from my perspective, but also clear directives for separate futures.

Perfectly packaged. Not so much a façade this time around, more of a saving face, for the message rings true to me, even now. We did love each other. We did desire different paths. We still do!

Looking back, it was the perfect end to our seemingly perfect courtship. Fit for Instagram but finally the truth–we were not meant to be.

P.S. Feel free to steal this text if ever you should need. Those who received it told me it was pure gold. Trust me.

IT IS WITH HEAVY HEARTS THAT
WE ARE NO LONGER GETTING MARRIED.
WE HAVE COME TO THE CONCLUSION THAT
WHILE WE HAVE AN ENORMOUS AMOUNT OF
LOVE AND RESPECT FOR EACH OTHER, WE WISH
TO TAKE DIFFERENT PATHS IN LIFE AND
THEREFORE ASK FOR YOUR CONTINUED LOVE
AND SUPPORT WHILE WE TAKE OUR SEPARATE
LIFE JOURNEYS.

WITH LOVE,

Katherine & Mr. Ex

Chapter 11

Unplanning

"Ruin is the road to transformation."

— Eat, Pray, Love

Wedding Countdown: One week to go
When you are publicly known for and privately quite proud of your perfect planning skills, unplanning a wedding is perhaps simpler, though far more gut-wrenching, than you might think.

Once I had informed the un-guests, it was time to take back control and unplan the rest. Not to spoil the punchline, but miraculously, with the help of the most amazing wedding planner and my savior on more than one occasion, The Wedding Planner Extraordinaire, and my incredible, wonderful, strong, intelligent, force-of-freaking-nature mother, we somehow managed to sort out the demise of my wedding within a few harried weeks.

Once alerted, The Wedding Planner Extraordinaire jumped in with two well-heeled feet and dealt swiftly with several vendors. Reviewing contracts with Mom and trying her best to recoup any loses, she canceled roughly six different contracts with swift efficiency.

All canceled.

But what about the rest of the bits involved in a wedding?

That was all Mom. Bow down to the Mother of the Bride. Like seriously, bow down to the Queen herself.

Ooooof! She had it tough.

* * *

Let's start with the location, The Broadmoor in Colorado Springs, Colorado.

Oh, the Broadmoor, *sigh,* with its sprawling gardens, palatial pastel-peach façade, private lake, outdoor terraces and extravagantly decorated ballrooms, mouth-watering restaurants galore, pubs, cocktail bars, and lounges, each with their own unique personality, and an all-around perfect natural backdrop nestled at the base of Cheyenne Mountain. Trust me when I say, it was supposed to be a dream.

Mom had the spectacularly unspectacular task of meeting with the esteemed Broadmoor event team to unplan as much as humanly possible. Like a United Nations global summit, she faced the various departmental heads who lead planning at the historic property, and they got to work. Food & Beverage, Reservations, Activities, they were all there, and the answer across the board was the same…

Pay up.

Contractually, we were indeed on the hook whether we had used it or not. No exceptions.

I'm not saying it was unfair. It wasn't. Like the bajillion dollar per year wedding industry as a whole, it was strictly business. Nothing personal.

So, what do you do with a previously paid in full wedding venue and accoutrements, yet no wedding? Apparently, you have a phenomenally weird party.

Anyone who couldn't cancel flights or simply wanted to take their long-planned vacay was invited to join my family for an intimate little non-wedding shindig to take place the same weekend as the wedding was supposed to.

We had to pay the band, after all, and they were supposed to be incredible!

I'm not sure how everyone felt about it, but in the end, there was at least entertainment for what was undoubtedly a very weird, but pretty darn fun party. At least so I heard. Hell no, I wasn't emotionally stable enough to be there. But friends and family of mine in attendance still rave about how much fun they had.

Either way, it was much ado about not much. Just a small group of family and friends, trying their best to celebrate amidst otherwise somber circumstances.

Celebrate what though...Life? Family? Togetherness? Love?

Mostly, I think each of them showed up to celebrate and support my mother. As hard as it was on me, the planning and unplanning process of my failed wedding was equally as challenging for Mom. Though I did not properly acknowledge it, or even notice at the time, looking back, I see her distress. Her daughter was relieved but broken-hearted, and there my mom was left holding the proverbial rice-filled exit bag. Proud as she was, it can't have been easy.

* * *

And then there were *les fleurs*.

In this very much out-of-control phase of life, I wanted to control anything I could. So, given my love of creating an amazing experience for other people to enjoy and a parallel desire to control the uncontrollable, I painstakingly crafted every detail of our wedding.

For the eleven long months leading up to our wedding date, I was single-mindedly obsessed with achieving a Pinterest-picture-perfect, blush and gold galore, all pink everything, fairytale princess meets modern romance wedding weekend.

My family are big time flower people, and my grandfather has the greenest thumb of anyone I've ever met. His backyard perpetually looks like the Garden of Eden, and he even keeps his own personal greenhouse to perfectly protect his collection of orchids from the unpredictable Oklahoma weather. From as early as I can even remember, I would help him and my grandmother plant bulbs, perennials, and other treasures in the garden each year. I would prune the ever-present rose bushes, pick weeds, and help gather the apples from their small apple tree on the side of the house. I spent hours in the garden, learning the names of all the varieties and began to be able to identify them on sight.

I lingered there even after the work was done, soaking up the unmistakable glory of being surrounded by true natural beauty, the soft perfume of the delicate blooms scenting the thick summer air. I can still smell the honeysuckle vines creeping up and over their back fence, enclosing me in its sweet, candied aroma.

Mom, too, is a flower fanatic. Having also learned from the best, she knows exactly what she likes and exactly where to find it. Fluffy, soft, full, and romantic, she can pick the most exquisite blooms and expertly combine them to create true works of art.

So, between my mother and me, you better believe the florals were going to be perfection.

Basically, picture Marie Antoinette's parties at the height of her ridiculousness and extravagance and you begin to get the picture of what I had planned.

It was definitely a vibe worthy of Pinterest boards around the world, but was it authentic?

I think not.

Truth...I will unapologetically love beautiful flowers for as long as I shall live, but what about the rest? In reality, in the cold, hard light of day, the gaudy and over-the-top design was not authentic to me.

Even worse, it wasn't a fantasy, it was fiction.

Yes, I do believe many brides get a little out of control when it comes to what we think we need for a wedding to be spectacular. For starters, it's about the couple and really nothing else should matter. But in this often self-indulgent phase of life, many can become hyper-focused on superfluous wedding fluff.

I was no different, but for me, it was worse. Our wedding was the exact visual depiction of the image that Mr. Ex desperately wanted us to portray. In his mind, there was no such thing as too much gold for this golden couple. And when it came down to it, the wedding was literally to be the gilded age reincarnated in every way possible, right down to the traditional gender roles and the false pretenses. It didn't resonate with my true self or my aspirations. However, it did accurately mirror the façade of my relationship with Mr. Ex. It was all for show.

Months after the wedding was called off, this railcar on the runaway train of deception was one of the pieces that pained and confounded me the most. Why did I let it get so out of control? How did I end up with something so fake? What was I trying to prove? Was it all for love? Was I trying to please Mr. Ex? Was I covering up my doubt with "stuff" to distract our guests from seeing the reality of our relationship? Were my decisions based in fear? Did being married, no matter the cost, really matter that much to me?

What the heck happened here?

For the longest time, I couldn't pin it down, but in the moments, hours, and years of reflecting since this season of my life, I've finally come to a conclusion–it was a disguise. A masquerade. A ruse. It was not just for the benefit of others, but worse, a deception to my own self. I was so desperately trying to hide from the truth I was willing to go to any length to present a *Martha Stewart Weddings*-worthy wedding.

I was terrified it would be a failure of a marriage, but I wasn't about to let the wedding show any sign of this uncertainty.

Feeling overwhelmed? Pink leather, laser-cut linens it is.

Crippled by doubt? Double the golden candlesticks. Triple it, even.

Anxiety so bad you can't breathe? More sparkle, people. More. More. More. More I say! Off with your head!

Gild the mask so much that nobody can see beyond the gleam, beyond the façade, beyond the fictional front. Camouflage this increasingly shrinking violet with a veneer of roses so thick she all but disappears. Drape the voile just so, so nobody will pay attention to the real woman behind the curtain.

Hide the truth at all costs.

It's a similar story to my wedding dress, I guess.

It wasn't my dress.

It wasn't my floral and decor.

It wasn't my truth.

It *was* my disguise.

It just took me eleven months and nineteen days to admit it to myself.

* * *

Over the years, the question I am asked second most frequently after the previously discussed *"How did you know?"* is, *"What did you do with your dress?"*

Usually my quippy response of "Which one?" makes us both laugh and gives me the perfect opportunity to artfully change the subject.

Yet, despite my avoidance, I do understand why this question is so intriguing. At some point in time, most women, and some men, have imagined themselves in a wedding dress. After all, it's the most expensive dress many of us will ever be lucky enough to wear.

So, finally, here is my answer to that question: I still have them…both of them.

I'm not sure why I found this answer shameful for so long. After all, I have a deep and undying love for fashion. Ever since I played dress up with my grandmother's '50s fashion, old faux fur shrugs, cocktail jewelry, and patent leather pumps, I have flat out been obsessed. So, naturally my obsession would extend to my wedding dresses. I mean, I have ZERO intention of ever wearing my ceremony dress, but it's been a little hard to part with a literal piece of art made to fit my body like a glove.

Nevertheless, admitting I couldn't quite part with my wedding dress? Definitely not a chic look.

Until recently, I had actually never even seen them in their final form. Once the wedding was off, I instructed Mom to pack them up in storage or put them in the vault, or really just stash them anywhere I wouldn't accidentally stumble upon them.

It was as if I thought they had special powers. Like somehow seeing them would magically undo all the healing and all the growth I was fighting so hard to create in my new life.

In all honesty, I think I was scared of them.

Maybe it's because they each have names. Like real names. I'm not making this up, nor did I name them myself. Many bridal dresses *actually* have human first names, bestowed upon them by their makers, like Geppetto and Pinocchio. They have personalities all their own, too, and in many ways, I guess brides are bound to look at them like "real girls."

We choose them not only based on who *they* are, but who they allow *us* to be when we wear them. If we're shy, the right dress supernaturally bestows us with confidence and self-assurance.

If we're clumsy, a classically tailored gown makes us graceful and elegant. If we lack overt sex appeal, well then, a well-cut frock makes us a matrimonial Marilyn, sensual and comfortable in our own skin.

All this power to transform, it's no wonder I was scared of *Lakely*.

You see, Lakely was my ill-fated ceremony gown and as I described before, she was fiieeeeerce y'all. As such, I had to lock her away until I was strong enough to resist her charms. After all, she was NOT meant for me. She was the faux-me, the pretend-me I fought so hard to break free from. She was the future I most certainly did not want, and I was damned if she would bring me back under her lacey French spell.

Mom recently unpacked the old gal, and it was odd, but Lakely was no longer the Lakely of old.

She was just a dress. A bundle of tulle, French lace, sequins, and satin. No special powers, no spell whatsoever.

For someone who has a genuine emotional reaction to beautiful clothes on a daily basis, my lack of response, while not altogether unexpected given my personal growth over the years, was a triumph.

I have evolved so far beyond this dress, I thought.

I have flourished and built a new life. A life that reflects my authentic and true self, and I love it. With all my heart, I love my life and who I get to be today.

So, it is finally time to say goodbye to this vestige of the past, and here's my pitch:

If you're a 5'9", short-torsoed, mostly legs, moderately well-endowed in the chest department (at least I was before breast feeding), roughly size four gal, then this dress is for you! Hit me up.

As for my Victorian-inspired, long-sleeved, lace and sheer tulle reception dress, she's all mine, baby. I'm manifesting an appropriately dark and gothic gala or costume ball I can wear this gem to one day. Or maybe a masquerade—one that this time, I'm excited to go to.

Chapter 12

The Weekend That Wasn't

"The world breaks everyone and afterward
many are strong at the broken places."
– Ernest Hemingway, *A Farewell to Arms*

*W*edding Countdown: Two days to go
June 15, 2019, was supposed to be the best day of
my life.

The beginning of my forever, my pinnacle of
achievement as an Oklahoma-born woman and the moment
I officially became Mrs. Ex. It was a goal I had been counting
down toward each and every day for months on end. My
wedding day was the be all, end all, and I genuinely could
not see beyond it. I dreamed it would be the most magical
Bridgerton meets *Pride and Prejudice* perfect moment I would
ever experience.

Now, two weeks post break up, instead of counting
down with anticipation, I was steeling myself to face the
very same day, which I was now dreading every minute of
every hour since the second we had called it off.

In truth, I wasn't quite sure how to feel about June 15.

Logically, it was likely to be a beautiful, summer
Colorado day just like any other. But emotionally?
Emotionally it felt like a ticking time bomb set to explode at

the exact hour of my almost wedding. Like somehow once that time passed, it was all a little more real and permanent, a little more final, a little more 'til death we have parted. Like once the wedding date came and went and we were not announced as man and wife, this long-idealized chapter of my life was well and truly closed. It was the end of my dream as I knew it.

As I said, I never really fantasized past the wedding. So now, I was getting ready to head into the wildly unknown territory of my new and terrifying future as the once again single, thirty-something me.

I was also pretty sure the passing of this milestone would officially kick in my grief reflex.

You see, I'm a processor, through and through. I need time to take in all the available information and roll it around in my brain for a few days before I fully allow myself the space to react and feel. Given the magnitude of the trauma I was dealing with, a few days just wasn't enough processing time, and I was still buffering more than ten days on, like the old school days of dial-up internet.

My situation still didn't quite seem real, and I knew once the fateful date was upon us, the reality would sink in like a red wine stain on a once-pristine ivory dress, and I would finally have to face the very, very, very big feelings I was fighting to keep at bay. The emotional starting gun was loaded, and I feared the arrival of my would-be wedding day would sound the starting shot.

For, despite my relief and continued commitment to my decision, there was in fact grief–tons and crushing tons of grief. Even though I now had the freedom I'd so desperately craved, I had still recently lost hugely important chunks of my life: my partner, my wedding, my future family, my pride, my reputation. *Poof*, and it was gone, but I was yet to grieve the loss of the life I had envisioned.

Regardless of what the first half of this book suggests, I HATE to cry in front of people. It is my literal worst nightmare. I used to feel it showed a level of weakness and vulnerability I was not comfortable presenting to the world, and I so did not want to publicly break down yet again on the day of my would-have-been wedding.

To save face and allow myself to cry in peaceful solitude like the normal, strong, and sane person I was trying to be, I decided to face this weekend alone. Solo, sad, and lonely, but safe from judgmental eyes.

Looking back now, I think I was following a decree of self-inflicted excommunication, fed by a secret desire to punish myself for the guilt I still felt over breaking up with Mr. Ex. I was also hoping I could finally force a wallow-fest to help me face my grief head on. Even then, I was still working out how much was too much "me time" and when I might need to call in reinforcements. I was waffling between surrounding myself with distractions and friends or hiding away like a proper hermit for the entire weekend. I truthfully didn't know how I needed to heal myself. I didn't know how I needed to grieve. I didn't know what I needed at all, and facing the weekend of June 15 was a whopper, to say the least.

Naturally, there was only one place in the entire world I could go. A singular place where I could escape the prying eyes of Oklahoma and Denver and feel like my most authentic self. My happy place. My sacred escape. My Zen garden and my mecca all rolled into one—our family cabin in Snowmass, Colorado.

My grandfather and grandmother built our cozy wood cabin in the 1970s and blissfully, not much has changed since then. All of my nearest and dearest memories have occurred at this house. Reading in my grandfather's favorite sunlit chair as elk, moose, bears, and every other woodland creature sauntered by, beautifully unphased by my voyeuristic gaze. Endless summers spent hiking the woods around the house with my little sister, pretending to be explorers in a foreign wilderness. Winter nights digging ice forts in the snow plow mounds at the end of the driveway until our mother forced us to come inside and warm our blue lips and bright red noses. Leaf peeping galore. Summer rainstorms resulting in that very specific "damp aspen trees after the rain" smell, which lets me know I'm in my personal heaven. It is truly my favorite place on this earth, so I figured all the place-specific joy and happy memories would help to soften the blow of my grief like a pillowy landing pad of positivity.

It was a perfect plan.

So, in the words of John Muir, "into the forest I go, to lose my mind and find my soul."

I drove up on the afternoon of Thursday, June 13, and as soon as I hopped out of the car onto our gravel driveway and inhaled *that* humid, earthy smell, I knew I was home. I unpacked and settled in for the turbulent weekend ahead and let myself lean into the loving embrace of our Snowmass home.

* * *

Wedding Countdown: One day to go

The next day, it was time for my most-cherished summer ritual, hiking in Maroon Bells.

The Maroon Bells mountains are named for the, you guessed it, wine-colored, bell-like formations in the Elk Mountain Range near Aspen, Colorado. These three craggy, 14,000-foot peaks are also nicknamed the Deadly Bells because of the difficulty level involved in summiting them, but to me, they are the warmest, most inviting, most beautiful place in Colorado.

I have been hiking the Bells since I was old enough to walk–my mom would take us out wandering there as children–and I guess I've felt connected ever since. I feel myself in the Bells, more at ease there than any other place on earth. There, I can breathe freely. I can release the pressures and the stress of whatever is going on in life and I can just *be*. Put simply, it is my soul's happy place.

Maroon Bells means so much to me that I even have a portrait of the mountains tattooed on my left foot so I can carry the way I feel there with me no matter where I go. Three hours of utter pain, but a lifetime reminder of the joy I feel when surrounded by the burgundy-hued Colorado wilderness.

Despite having completed the hike from Maroon Lake to Crater Lake about a million times in my life, (I even hiked it again the day before I edited this chapter, so I could power-up my mountain love), no two hikes are ever the same. I am a different person, in a different circumstance each time I scale those beautiful Bells and thus, I learn and feel something new each time as well. Given my current state, I wasn't sure what to expect from myself on the journey this time around, but I knew I needed to do the short trek nonetheless. I needed to face it, whatever *it* was. I was optimistic the hike would somehow heal some small part of me, and I was willing to sacrifice my pain to the mountains, if they would have me that is.

So off I set, climbing up and up and up. Moving at a mellow clip at first, I began to pick up speed. It felt like some unseen force was pushing me forward. "Faster. Stronger," it whispered. "You got this," the hidden power said as I continued to push myself to the limit, running now as I scaled the steepest bits. I ran harder, not daring to stop, for fear of being left behind by my veiled companion, my guide.

As I ran in a trance-like state, I began to think about the pace of life. Just like this hike, some stretches of life are steep and rocky and seriously tough. Some phases push you to your limit and make you feel like you can't even catch your breath, no matter how hard you try. This was the mental life phase I was in, and I think that's why I was pushing so hard in my physical body.

I needed to push through a challenge I KNEW I could conquer in order to give me the strength and confidence to conquer the unknown challenges awaiting me in my personal life back home. I needed to get to the beauty at the end of the effort, believe it was all worth it, and restore my hope. The lifelong hope that I might also one day be rewarded with an equally as beautiful love–a perfect, honest, true, big love–if only I could push through this season of the climb. I had to grasp that all I was going through was worth it, and let me tell you, it was.

Crater Lake, with its small, glassy surface reflecting the snow-capped Bells even in the heart of summer, reed-covered banks, and gently sloping hills where you can nap, recover, and receive all that nature has to offer, is truly an alpine beauty. For me, it is peace personified. It is and always has been the embodiment of the metaphorical pot of gold at the end of my rainbow.

As I summited the last saddle, I slowed my gait to a walk and strolled leisurely down to the shores of the lake. Finding a smooth, worn log, I dropped my pack to the ground and sat my weary, sweat-drenched self upon my makeshift seat. Once settled, I exhaled a deep, reverberating breath. A proper sigh of relief. My shoulders dropped. My fists unclenched. The long-held tension in my neck released as I rolled it gently from side to side. I breathed in as I lifted my head to the sky and couldn't help but smile as the gentle rays warmed my face.

I made it, I thought.

Basking in the shared joy of my fellow hikers relaxing lakeside, I was genuinely gleeful. Just like I had dropped my pack, I felt like I might also be capable of putting down my grief. For just a moment, I could take off the mantle of shame, guilt, and pain that had been the albatross tight around my neck, and I laid all my negative emotions at the altar of the Deadly Bells.

I acknowledged them.

I named them.

I expressed my gratitude for them.

I bid them farewell. And though I knew I would inevitably pack a few of them back into my hiking bag for the wander back to reality, I was also certain this time, the load would be lightened. This time, the load would be bearable. Ever so slightly, the grief was more manageable. The pain, less acute. The shame, smaller.

The Bells had quelled the torment of my soul.

Hiked out and happy, I drove back to the house. I had made it through almost an entire day of what should have been our wedding weekend successfully, but unfortunately for me, things were about to take a turn for the worse.

The Friday night of our welcome party, an event I had been planning almost as much as the wedding itself, was officially upon me. I started to picture guests arriving and imagined how I would have greeted them.

I pictured the Beverly Hills Hotel décor I had painstakingly perfected, and I imagined the cool taste of the pale pink frosé as it slipped through my perfectly painted lips. The laughter of friends and family echoed in my mind as they played games outside on the lawn, chatted excitedly, and wished Mr. Ex and I well for the days to follow. I saw it all like a virtual reality, and then I saw it slowly fade to black. It was all a wistful dream. In reality, I was alone in an isolated cabin in the woods. Completely stinking alone.

I had already completed the pre-planned mountain activities I had been counting on to distract me from my depressing reality, and now all I had to look forward to was two more nights of cooking for one at home, and perhaps a walk or two. Not quite the refuge I was hoping for.

Desperately lonely and sadder by the second, I did what any millennial would do: I began posting "happy" selfies on social media. I posted photos of my spandex-clad self doing yoga poses all over the Bells, embarrassingly thirsty bikini pics of me in the hot tub on our deck, and sultry pics of me cooking in the kitchen. What is a sultry cooking pic, you ask? Great question; all I know is they weren't great. If that's not a cry for attention, then I don't know what is.

The responses were flattering and supportive, but unsurprisingly, one of my besties saw past the façade and reached out in earnest. The Blonde One was officially on the case!

Oddly enough, we became friends because Mr. Ex was friends with The Blonde One's then boyfriend, but when the time came, she stood by my side as a pillar of support. For as long as I'd known her, her quirky, kind, and thoughtful energy was exactly what I needed. I was in good hands.

Not to mention the fact that she had already carried the burden of my despair for two weeks, and yet, she remained undeterred. She was my party partner for the first few days after I called it off and my sleepover mate while we pretended we were back in middle school. She was my shoulder to cry on and sounding board, and she wasn't even done yet.

Totally unbeknownst to me, The Blonde One decided that despite my protests, I should NOT be alone on the day of my wedding. And so, she immediately packed up her car and started the four-hour drive from Denver to Snowmass. No questions asked, wouldn't take no for answer, she quite literally rode to my rescue. As she rolled in late Friday night, she found a now mostly drunk me still lounging on the leather sofa in a wet bikini and promptly put me to bed. Then she hatched a plan for the impending doomsday to come, otherwise known as my should-have-been, almost, close-but-not-quite wedding day.

* * *

Wedding Countdown: Zero days to go

The next morning, The Blonde One miraculously discovered that the Snowmass Food & Wine Festival was happening on the mountain that day, so we figured it was the ideal distraction.

Take endless food, endless drinks, a bunch of strangers to chat to briefly but zero risk of conversations that get too deep, and you have yourself a winning recipe for how to avoid thinking about your wedding. Those kinds of events are also a fertile ground for opportunities to flirt, and I'll admit, I needed a little confidence boost courtesy of some good old fashioned flirting, even if it was surface at best.

The Blonde One and I got all gussied up in our effortlessly chic, but also a touch bohemian, Colorado food festival attire and prepared to enter the fray.

I chose a floor length wrap maxi dress of royal blue silk with bright white polka dots. I LOVE a polka dot moment. They are flirty and romantic, yet reserved and elegant. At least to me.

It had a deep-V neckline down to there and flutter sleeves, so I felt the abundant décolletage was offset by the otherwise full body coverage. I'd also recently chopped my hair into an angular bob and dyed it bright white–not just platinum blonde, even whiter–and I loved my new hair, too. It was fun, fearless, and more than a smidge edgy. It was the perfect match for the attitude I was trying to embrace. I looked like a cartoon villain (see Mirage from *The Incredibles*), but it was epic.

Ready to roll, we took one of the three Ubers running in Snowmass Village and waltzed into the party. Bluegrass music played loudly over the speakers with a conversational buzz solidly holding up the background beat. Full-bellied laughter punctuated the summer sonata, and the overall effect was uplifting and bright. The sun shone warmly on us all.

We assessed the scene and began our perusal of the various vendor tents scattered in a circle about the grassy knoll. Barbecued ribs and smoked pork butt, champagne, ceviche and fish tacos, custom grills, wine of every flavor, color, and variety, grilled summer corn elote, and so much more. It was a feast for our eyes, mouths, and souls alike! We gorged ourselves on anything we could reach, and when we were full, we went back for more.

We were really getting in the swing of things when I accidentally bumped into a total stranger, who, when he turned around, turned out not to be a total stranger at all. It was Mr. Aspen Ski Co himself, a former colleague of mine from when I did marketing for Colorado Ski Country USA, Colorado's not-for-profit trade association that, at the time, represented twenty-one different ski areas throughout the state.

Now, when I tell you I loved that job, I'm not being facetious. I LOVED THAT JOB. I loved my team. I loved our office culture. I loved the industry. I loved the people I met across the state who not only ran the front offices of the resorts, but even more so, the guys and gals who worked behind the scenes to keep the ski areas going strong. The groomers, the snowmakers, the terrain park builders–in short, the operations folks who make the mountains what we know and love.

I LOVED THOSE GUYS. Working with them to plan the annual Snow Conference was and will always be a highlight of my time at Ski Country, and it just so happened that Mr. Aspen Ski Co was my greatest ally in those efforts. He'd backed me up when others had discounted me as the token woman in the room. He was a mentor on the operations side of the industry, and he was a helluva lot of fun to boot. Not to mention the fact that he perpetually offered me a job, which was ultimately the best compliment of all.

All this to say, when Mr. Aspen Ski Co turned around, we were both equally shocked and elated. I'd left my role at Ski Country about a year prior, so our reunion was equal parts long overdue and welcome. We jumped right in, catching up, hearing about each other's families, doing a quick recap of our mutual acquaintances since I'd left, and then we got to the big ole question that hung heavy in the air like clouds pregnant with rain: "How was the wedding?!"

I must have momentarily let my face betray me, because almost as soon as the question left his lips, Mr. Aspen Ski Co quickly followed up with a somber and sincere, "Oh no, tell me everything."

I went blank at that point because I have absolutely no idea how I described the situation, other than managing to explain that not only had I called the wedding off two weeks prior, but today, yes, *today*, was the day we were supposed to get married.

Mr. Aspen Ski Co listened intently, then clapped me on the back like the older brother type he's always been and said simply, "Congratulations."

That was it; he just knew. He knew Mr. Ex had been the wrong guy, and even more, he supported me completely and totally without judgment. I think he was even a smidge proud of his little Snow Conference protégé, and in that moment, I was willing to accept his praise. It was the literal pat on the back I needed to keep my chin up, raise another glass, and embrace the bluegrass music ringing out across the crowd.

It was a tough day, but Mr. Aspen Ski Co reminded me I was a tough gal.

I really do got this, I thought as I hugged him warmly and continued our girl gang tour of the food tents.

Eventually we had our fill of the festival and called it quits for the day. We headed home and did what any single thirty-something would do after a day of eating and drinking: we immediately changed into swimsuits and hopped in the hot tub! We cranked the radio and relaxed into the jets of the bubbling bath. What a blissful day. I was with my friend, I was in the mountains, and I was blessed beyond belief. I was almost blissed out enough that I didn't even notice as the ceremony time crept closer and closer.

Almost.

4:00 p.m. came and went, and it was manageable.

4:15 p.m. passed by and though I felt the sadness beginning to creep in, I kept it at bay.

4:30 p.m. rolled on by and I knew I was in trouble.

Then, at 4:38 p.m. MST on June 15, 2019, the proverbial door officially closed.

I will never forget that exact moment, for, based on my knowledge of the length of the pre-vow message, our vows, the prayers, etc., I knew this was the moment when we would have been announced as Mr. and Mrs. Ex. This would have been the start of our forever. This would have marked the achievement of my ultimate goal. And instead, I was sitting in a hot tub with The Blonde One trying desperately not to cry.

Coincidentally, it was pouring in Colorado Springs, so there was a marginal cosmic win, I guess.

Yet, despite the relief and happiness I *was* feeling, I was suddenly overcome with pain, grief, and guilt. I couldn't hold it together anymore and the only way I can describe it is that a switch flipped. I downed the last of my champagne and I was gone. Checked out. Blacked out. Call it what you want. I had well and truly left the building.

I don't remember exactly how it went down (recall the long day at the festival), but I do recall I turned into a total jerk. Pardon my French, but I was a complete asshole the rest of the evening, and I directed this assholiness at the one person who deserved it the least, The Blonde One.

Now, I'm a firm believer that grief and sadness and difficult life circumstances never give you carte blanche to be rude to your friends. They are there for you, even when they have their own life stuff happening, and I wouldn't be the person I am if I thought my personal baggage gave me the right to be rude to others or hurt their feelings. Thus, I'm ashamed to admit, given the circumstances, that being a jerk to my wonderful friend was exactly what I did.

I broke one of my own cardinal rules, and I can still feel the hurt I caused her. Instead of meeting her overt kindness with my own gratitude, I was sharp, harsh, and cutting. What's worse is I didn't even realize it at the time. In my temporary madness, I didn't mentally clock I was hurting her, but sure enough, the next day, after we had slowly made our way back to Denver, she had the guts to tell me how she felt. She told me the brutal and honest truth about how drunk I had been and how I'd treated her, how I'd hurt her, and though it stung in the worst possible way, it was exactly what I deserved. I had let my own hurt cause me to wound one of the friends I love most in this world, and she stepped up to tell me to cut that crap out.

She was right.

I am so grateful The Blonde One cared enough about our relationship to say something, to be brutally honest, to be a friend. She didn't tell me what I *wanted* to hear, she told me what I *needed* to hear, and it was the best thing that has ever happened in our friendship. From there, we've miraculously continued to grow in our ability to communicate as friends and as women.

More importantly, though, it served as an invaluable lesson for the challenging months ahead of exactly how NOT to act. Despite my chaotic mess of a life, I had no right to treat people poorly. Just because hurt people often hurt people doesn't mean they should. I believe in my core that people deserve love and respect, and I needed to be reminded of this central pillar of my life. In the fray of calling it off, I had lost that part of myself.

It was also the wake-up call I needed to reign in the drinking once and for all. I could make excuses for using alcohol as a self-destructive crutch while I was still engaged and miserable and trying to numb out. But if I really wanted to heal, I'd need to throw my crutch to the wayside. I wanted to move forward and develop a healthy relationship with both myself and others, and to do so, my relationship with alcohol also needed to mend.

Right then and there I decided to re-evaluate how I healed.

From then on, no more drunken escapism, no more rants to friends, no more relying on anything or anyone but myself.

It was time to come back to my true self. Back to the version of me *I* loved and respected.

Tough love wins again.

Chapter 13

Uncoupling

"We suffer more often in imagination than in reality."
– Lucius Annaeus Seneca

Wedding Countdown: One week after

To me, one of the most difficult aspects of a breakup isn't even the split from your former number one person–it's the chasm that results between you and the *entire* social circle you and your bf/gf constructed together over years of shared experiences. The group of souls you collectively invited into your private lives. The comrades you laughed, partied, danced, cried, wandered, and generally lived life with for however many years your partnership with your ex flourished.

In my experience, when a breakup happens, the friend group members tend to follow one particular strategy. In said strategy, shared couple friends assure you neither of them will take sides, because they "love you both so much." Then, they do take sides and whatever gender has the "better" or longer friendship, he or she gets the entire couple. So, if the dude is closer to your ex, he gets the couple in full. But if you are closer to the gal, you get the pairing all to yourself. Of course, there are exceptions to every rule, but you get the gist.

Given this gendered split, though, it also typically means a good number of the girl gang you met through your significant other will disappear, leaving you to face about six million additional friend breakups as your former friends are forced to take your ex's side. And this is a best-case scenario when it's an amicable breakup situation.

Consider the fact that I broke up a wedding (not exactly amicable by anyone's definition) and you can probably imagine when it came to choosing sides, the majority of our joint friend group sided promptly with Mr. Ex. Not all of them, mind you, but enough to leave a giant void in my heart.

These were people I, too, loved and respected and shared endless memories with. And yet, when they walked away from me, despite the heartache I felt, I understood why they did it. They were caught between a rock and a hard place, and I have never blamed them for choosing to support Mr. Ex throughout our saga. But, damn, did it hurt like the dickens.

So, without further ado, this is how our uncoupling went down...

Out of respect for Mr. Ex and perhaps fear of experiencing our mutual friends' reactions firsthand, I let Mr. Ex communicate our breakup with almost every single one of our shared friend group. Whether he'd brought the couple into our life or not, I felt so guilty that I let him take the first crack at claiming them, and he did, one by gut-wrenching one.

Any and all single males? As one would expect, they ran precipitously to Mr. Ex's camp. Even worse, not only did they make their allegiance known, but they were also properly brutal in how they showed their team colors. They could have silently ghosted me like normal humans. I could have easily handled said tactic, but some took it a hurtful step further. I will forever remember one interaction in particular.

I was about forty-five minutes into an elliptical session at our shared local gym when I saw Mr. Gym Bro–so named for his obvious hours in the gym–walk in the front door. He had been the focus of some pretty serious accusations recently, and I'd defended him tooth and nail. So, I hoped my allegiance to him in his time of need might mean we could still be on speaking terms during my struggles as well.

As he walked my way, I stared straight at him with a full, cheesy smile, hoping to say hello. He strolled closer and closer, but when he didn't so much as glance my direction, I thought, *Oh, he must not see me,* and began waving enthusiastically.

No head nod, no wave, not even the slightest eye twitch to show his recognition. He flat out ignored me. Truly dejected, I consoled myself by reiterating that he must not have seen my wave, but I knew the truth. I knew it was the first of many brush offs and "see ya later sisters" to be flung callously my way. It was my first banishment from the group, and I was completely unprepared for such a blatant slap in the face. So much so that I refused to go back to the gym for weeks out of fear I might face Mr. Gym Bro once more.

As they say, the first is always the worst. And it was. But it definitely wasn't the last.

The one bright spot in the whole single male friend group exodus was Mr. Electronic Dance Music (aka Mr. EDM). Throughout our friendship, we'd always shared an easy, fun, and witty banter. We genuinely got along well, but he was Mr. Ex's bestie, so I assumed he would be team Bros Before Hoes. Never in a million years did I expect him to be the one to step up and reach out to comfort me, but in a shocking twist of fate, he was.

Mr. EDM surprised the hell out of me when, a few days after the Big Day, he sent me a message on Instagram to ask how I was holding up. It wasn't much in the way of conversation starters, but it was a lifeline and an acknowledgment that I was, in fact, still welcome to be a participant in his life. It let me know I still mattered to him, even in some small way. We wouldn't stay close per se, but to this day, we still exchange an occasional DM. A heart to my story here, a crying laughing face emoji there, sometimes a few sentences back and forth. It's not a lot, and he certainly remains firmly by Mr. Ex's side, but his kindness and continued connection is meaningful to me, nonetheless. I can only assume he recognized I was trying to do right by both my and Mr. Ex's happiness, and so, he gave me grace. In contrast to Mr. Gym Bro, Mr. EDM was my reminder to accept blessings and celebrate small wins, from wherever and whenever they may come.

Another set of folks we had to uncouple was–you guessed it–our couple friends. As I stated before, typically, the girls stick with the girls and the guys ride with the guys. It's a pretty simple party line. In my case, it was once again a bit trickier as I let my own personal shame and guilt get in the way of recognizing who actually WAS on my side the whole time.

To my surprise, most of the couples I was truly close with committed to staying friends with both of us. It wasn't just lip service, either: they went out of their way to show their support with actions, calls, notices of group outings, invites to birthday parties, and the like for both Mr. Ex and me. They showed me I did not need to opt out of events or remove them from my must-call list, but I did, anyway, because I was terrified of answering questions. I was ashamed I had portrayed the false façade for so long. I felt guilty for choosing myself. I was a total mess trying to heal and put the pieces of my broken life back together, and I didn't want those happy, thriving couples to see my suffering. I didn't necessarily want to run into Mr. Ex at a group function just yet, either.

So, what did I do? I rebuffed almost all of their caring and kind advances, no doubt hurting them in the process as well.

You remember The Blonde One, who literally rode to my rescue in Aspen on the weekend of my wedding? She was an exception. As you've already seen, she showed up for me in the biggest and best ways possible, and she and I remain close to this day.

But the rest of the couple friends? The rest I could not bring myself to face. I turned down events. I stopped answering texts. I ghosted. I declined. I pushed *them* away. I had spent the last two years cultivating these relationships, building bridges and shared connections, and yet now, I ran. Here they were, showing up for me in my darkest hours, and I couldn't reciprocate.

One-way streets can only be driven for so long, and over time, we all drifted apart. Still, my love for them remains. They are incredible humans, and I religiously follow their lives on social media, silently celebrating their marriages, pregnancies, new home purchases, and promotions with nothing but joy and encouragement. It still saddens me I am not there in person to hug them and tell them "congrats!" but all hope is not lost. Many of them still send the occasional Bat-Signal my way in the hopes I will once again rejoin their lives and the friendships we built.

In the end, I didn't need to lose as many friendships as I did. I let my fear, shame, and self-flagellation get the better of me, and it was devastating. Even so, I would do it all over again. For even with my mass uncoupling from my friends, it was nothing compared to the alternative of being stuck in an unhappy marriage, unfulfilled and untrue to myself.

I always knew I chose myself over Mr. Ex. I knew it from moment one. Though as I reflect back now, I realize it probably felt like I also chose myself over my friends.

Maybe it wasn't my only option, but in that season of life, it felt like it was. I had to continually choose myself, my truth, my future. Not in the selfish way it sounds, but by consistently putting myself first and doing it with conviction. I had to see my decision through, and as terrifying and alienating as it was, I will never regret it. I did what I had to do to make it through the fire, and while I can apologize for the additional hurt I caused my friends in the process, I would brave it all again.

* * *

Beyond the physical friends, we also had to uncouple our digital lives as well. OK, I know what you're thinking: why on earth are you having an entire sub-section on social media? Well, let me tell you, when you put your entire relationship, and your entire life for that matter, on Instagram, people will notice when the long-anticipated wedding magically does *not* appear on your grid.

It's best to be prepared.

To the best of my memory, I waited about a week before I made any meaningful changes to my Instagram. Though Mr. Ex blocked me right away, I wasn't ready to make a public pronouncement to the World Wide Web.

When the time ultimately came, I did what many people do after a breakup—I changed my profile picture to a solo photo of me looking half-decent and deleted all past photos of Mr. Ex and me from my grid. One solid hour of effort, and I'd erased almost all evidence of our relationship from my public persona. Sure, it was like ripping off a really sticky, week-old bandage, pulling off both arm hair and little bits of skin, and I cried the whole time, but once it was finished, I really did feel better.

At least until the trolls came calling from under their digital bridges.

I swear, there is no better place to sniff out a breakup than on someone's well-curated Instagram feed. We see it time and time again in the celebrity gossip mags, and the same pattern holds true for us laypersons. When you see a sudden change in who is, or rather, who is not included on socials, you know something is amiss. The same was accurate for me. There was blood in the water, and I had unwittingly thrown the stinky, chunky bucket of chum in myself.

Needless to say, the rumor mill went wild.

Anyone who had not been invited to the wedding suddenly needed every intimate detail of what happened. Despite the fact they had absolutely zero right to this knowledge, I continuously received some version of the following inquiry:

"Did you postpone the wedding (apologies for asking)?"

Um...you're joking right?

Let me reiterate for those still learning this life lesson: if you have to apologize for asking, you clearly know better than to ask in the first place.

I wish I could say these hurtful inquiries were a few isolated incidents, but they weren't. Day after day, week after week, I all but went insane with peripheral acquaintances reaching out to get the details. Clearly my party line, despite its truth, of "we just weren't meant for each other" wasn't cutting it. People wanted more. They wanted every last drop of blood and guts and every last ounce of my devastatingly fragile sanity with it.

But just in case nobody else has told you yet, you don't owe the trolls anything! There is no price you need to pay to cross the bridge to your own healing and there is no right for them to charge for safe passage in the first place.

This is your story, your truth, and your decision, and you don't owe jack to anyone.

* * *

After tackling the friend group and my social media profile, the final piece of the uncoupling left to tackle was "The Stuff." When you spend two-plus years together, you are bound to accumulate your fair share of relationship paraphernalia. Add in wedding gifts and wedding favors and all the other inevitable trinkets couples gather like magpies, and The Stuff itself was overwhelming.

So, like I did when tackling the stuff of my uncoupling, let's start with the "easy" bits—also known as the unboxed and unused wedding gifts in a pile in the corner of the guest bedroom. Packages of all shapes and sizes, they just sat there like a set of building blocks intended to build the life of a future unrealized.

I truly hate to admit this, as I do not want to seem ungrateful for the time and money our loved ones spent selecting the most thoughtful and beautiful presents to celebrate our wedding. I am still touched by people's generosity. But, in order to explain this piece of the puzzle, I have to come clean. I flat out refused to unpack a single wedding gift we received in the three or four months leading up to the wedding.

A box would arrive, I would read the note and the packing slip to determine what life-building kitchen wares had arrived, enter the sender and item details into my wedding gift tracking spreadsheet so I could make sure to write a proper thank you note down the line, and then close the lid and add it to the pile in the corner. True, the guest room was a bit of a staging area for all things wedding, but when it came to wedding gifts, I refused to engage.

I told Mr. Ex my bizarre behavior was because I didn't have time to break down all of the boxes for recycling. And that is partially true. Anyone who has had the privilege of unpacking wedding gifts knows unboxing can be a daunting task. But in my heart of hearts, I didn't unpack them because I knew I might be returning them some time very soon. Ever the pragmatist, I guess I figured if I did need to return them all to sender, it would be far easier to do so if they were still in their original packaging.

After I called it off, their unavoidable presence was a reminder of a heartbreaking chapter in my currently crumbled life. I was keen to turn the page on this sorrow and get back to rebuilding without the stuff of the future I had fled, and as such, I needed to get the gifts out, and fast.

Some of them were actually pretty easy. All I had to do was go online, login to my registry for said store, click return, print the label, and drop off the reminder of our fiasco at the nearest shipping outlet. No muss, no fuss.

Then there were the remaining items I had selected from Williams Sonoma. *Gulp.*

After searching for online return options to no avail–rat farts!–I discovered I would need to return the gifts to the nearest Williams Sonoma location...in person. *Double gulp.*

I like to think I'm pretty good at knowing how to handle most social situations with grace, but I was at a loss for how "The Great Return" should go down. Did I walk up to the desk with my arms full of gifts and say, "I need to return these, please?" Did I lead with the entire story up front with something like, "I was engaged and then about a week ago I called my wedding off and now my life is a mess and I'm kinda depressed, and all this stuff is making it worse and I need to get it the hell out of my guest bedroom and can you please help me and just take it and make it all go away, thanks?"

I was certain this was not the right approach, but I was still lost on how to make my plea with something a little less cringy and unhinged. Would they ask the reason why I needed to return them? Would they somehow read the situation, show mercy upon my soul, and take them back no questions asked? Would they make me sit there and go through each item, one by one, until I slowly died of embarrassment right there on the spot?

"Oh, Lord, help me," I prayed as I pulled my wedding-gift-laden car up to the third floor of the Cherry Creek Mall parking garage.

Given that I could not possibly carry the cumbersome boxes with my own two hands, I waited until opening time, marched to the front door of Williams Sonoma, and promptly knocked on the storefront. Jared (yes, this is his real name, because if he ever reads this, he deserves a massive shout out!) unlocked the door and asked how he could help. This was my moment!

"I have a car full of wedding gifts I need to return because I called off my wedding. Can you help me?"

Short, sweet, and to the point. Not too rambly, but also a genuine and heartfelt plea for help. I felt like I nailed it.

I think he heard the desperation in my voice, and he replied kindly, "Of course. Let me grab some trolleys and I can come out to the car with you and help load them up. Give me a quick second to tell my associate where I'm going."

He smiled, nodded, and walked away assertively to get the chariots we would use to return the spoils of wedding war. When he returned, he pushed one gently toward me and told me to "lead the way."

On our way to my car, he asked genuinely, "How ya holdin' up?"

"Fine," I said, but then added more softly, "I mean it's obviously tough, you know, but I'm glad to be able to at least get this part done today."

"I get it," he said as we continued our march to the parking lot in silence.

We unloaded my car without much excitement and Tetrised the gifts well enough so they all miraculously fit on only two carts. "Phew," Jared said, "that was a close one."

You have no idea how close, I thought as I caught myself chuckling a bit out loud.

We slowly proceeded back to the store, and since it was still early on a weekday, not a soul was around to witness my embarrassing ordeal. I had hoped this would be the case, hence my 9:00 a.m. arrival, so I was glad to see at least some things could still go to plan.

Jared showed me where to park the carts and then resumed his place behind the counter so we could get down to business.

"What's the name on the registry?" he asked.

"Katherine Rose."

"And can you confirm the date of the wedding?"

"June 15, 2019," I confirmed.

"Oh my gosh, no way!" he said suddenly.

"What's wrong?!?" I asked, concerned I had somehow made some major faux pas.

"Oh no, nothing is wrong. You're just the second bride this week who has called off her wedding for that date."

"Huh," I offered. "I guess it wasn't a good day for weddings after all."

"Sure wasn't," he said, smiling.

Within two minutes, Jared had all the information he needed from me and told me I was free to go.

"That's it?" I asked, truly shocked I was getting off so easy.

"That's it," he said. "I'll scan everything later, but you don't need to wait around. I'll take care of it."

Bless you, Jared, I thought as I said, "Oh my goodness, thank you so much! I cannot tell you how much I appreciate you."

He smiled and offered a simple, "Anytime."

And with that, it was done.

I was free to go.

I walked back to my car in the bowels of the cavernous mall parking garage, closed the door, bowed my head, and cried. Not full-on sobs, but enough for the tears to leave streaks down my cheeks.

Why the melodramatic waterworks, you ask? After all, it was just The Stuff. Just things that not only did I never use but never even unpacked, so why was I crying alone in my car?

I'll tell you why it got to me…it wasn't about the things themselves. It was because they were all of The Things (proper noun, capital T things) Mr. Ex and I were going to use to build our home together, our future, our life. A life that was no longer happening and a future that, though it was supremely flawed, was a known entity. There was a part of me that mourned that life, that identity, and that future. A part of me still wondered if I had made the right decision to walk away and a part of me was still terrified of the unknown path before me.

And yet, despite the fear still sitting in the passenger seat beside me, ridding myself of those Things was also the shaking off of another shackle binding me to the past. It was a symbol of my commitment to moving forward and moving one step closer to a new life I could build, with new stuff, yes, but more importantly with new authenticity and hopefully one day a happily-ever-after love.

So you see, it was a letting go–a release–and the tears I cried were not of sadness, but of relief.

* * *

Now for far and away the worst part of our uncoupling…the day Mr. Ex finally moved out.

As you might expect, Mr. Ex and I were not really communicating much by this time. He would come and go, and sometimes take a box of his belongings, but he never told me in advance the exact date he planned to finalize his move. I simply walked upstairs to the guest bedroom one day and he was gone.

Clothes gone. Shaving kit gone. Gaming system gone. Truck gone.

All of him, totally and completely gone.

Of course, there were remnants left behind. The dirty sheets strewn about that smelled uniquely of him, his half-drunk water glass perched precariously on the windowsill, still-wet towels from his last shower in our home. Little bits of his memory, each one fading by the moment.

Now, it's one thing to know someone is moving, but it's quite another thing altogether when someone actually leaves forever. Even if you are the one who broke it off, the move out can still be abrupt and jarring and totally and completely overwhelming, and that's exactly what I felt the moment I realized he was gone for good. The surprise of this confirmation stopped me dead in my tracks and, you guessed it, I cried. There was a lot of crying in those first few weeks.

I collapsed to the floor as my knees buckled out from under me, too emotionally exhausted to stand, and I stared blankly around the room. *How on earth do I put all of this back together?* I thought. *Where do I start?* The thoughts swirling through my head were dizzying, and I legitimately thought I might pass out.

I shifted to lay flat on the floor, and I used all my strength to focus solely on the feeling of the ground beneath me. I felt each point where my body touched the floor, focusing on the sensation of connection between my flesh and the earth, focusing on any feeling that could bring me back to myself. I focused on the present breath, in and out, in and out, and nothing beyond the rhythmic rise and fall of my racing chest. Praying for centeredness, I lay there for what felt like an eternity, until mercifully my breath returned, and the hazy curtain of panic parted from behind my eyes. Taking a giant, deep breath, I was somehow able to answer my own question from many minutes before.

Where do I start? I thought again.

"It doesn't matter," I heard myself say aloud this time. "Just start."

And so, I did.

I stood up, tidied the towels into a cotton-clad bundle, stripped the bed, and threw every last linen into a pile bound for the laundry machine. I took the glasses and trash downstairs, sprayed the room with Febreze, and wiped down the bathroom surfaces, removing every last watermark I could find. When I finished my frenzy and turned around to survey the now very clean and almost empty room, I breathed a heavy sigh of relief. Cleaning always makes me happy, or perhaps more accurately, cleansing does, so the physical act of clearing space had an immediate impact upon my mood.

Energized and emboldened by my progress, I figured it would be a waste of personal momentum to stop now, so I continued on.

I collected every single picture frame off the walls and side tables and kitchen counter and bedside table and office desk that held a photo of Mr. Ex and me and stacked them on the dining room table before carefully removing the photos and placing each one delicately in a pile.

I sorted every shelf of knickknacks and pulled down any artifact of one of our trips, memories, and/or life together. I hauled it all into another large pile at my workstation and then carefully placed each item in one of two small boxes. One wood, one cardboard. Curious that I still remember this detail, but I do. *Shrug.*

There it was, our whole life, reduced down to two boxes of The Stuff.

Flowers we'd dried and saved, a champagne bottle and cork from our engagement trip, ticket stubs, plane tickets, hotel room keys, monogrammed cocktail napkins, game day lanyards, lava rocks, seashells from his family's home in Florida, not to mention all of the things I had ordered for the wedding. All of The Stuff, carefully cataloged and preserved.

I stepped back and assessed my handy work. And yet, I wasn't sure what to do next. I had two neat and tidy boxes, but now what?

"Do I toss it all in the trash?" Too harsh.

"Do I put it in my garage and risk its ruin in the unpredictable Colorado weather?" Too risky.

"Do I keep it in the house where it's safe, but I still have to look at it all the time?" Too close for comfort.

I couldn't just discard it, for throwing it away felt dismissive and overly reactive, and honestly, I just wasn't quite ready for said level of finality. I didn't want it to be destroyed, but I certainly did not want it laying around in eyesight every day, either.

"Storage it is," I decided aloud.

I tucked my two little boxes away in the far back left corner of my storage space and bid them adieu. Hiding them away like the Half-Blood Prince's potions book in the

Room of Requirement... (if you don't get the *Harry Potter* reference, take this as your sign to go watch that classic!), I pushed The Stuff out of my house and out of my mind for good.

Proud, relieved, and tired but inspired, I decided to address the reorganizational needs of the house as a whole. It felt duplicative to do the job halfway now and all the way later, so I dove in headfirst. I rearranged the gear in the garage, tidied my luggage, decluttered the closet, cleansed the workout-wear drawer, pared down my jeans, all of it. You name it, I systematized it and donated the lot. I revamped it all in an attempt to make my house my own again. My own perfect, comfortable, reflective, authentic space.

Only now, it wasn't just my couch as my safe haven, it was my entire home, and it was mine. All mine.

Chapter 14

The Very Merry Un-Honeymoon

"Who is the happier man, he who has braved the storm
of life and lived or he who has stayed securely
on shore and merely existed."
– Hunter S. Thompson

Wedding Countdown: Two weeks after
*Question: What do you do with your prepaid
honeymoon after you cancel the wedding of your dreams?*

Do you cancel it outright?

Do you audible and shift the excursion to another
remote destination so you only have to pay the still
substantial but not quite as horrible as full price change
fees?

Do you suck it up and go on your honeymoon alone?

Do you bolster yourself and take an emotional support
friend with you?

What the heck do you do when you have a full-fledged
honeymoon but no bride and groom?

*Answer: In my opinion, you grab your bestie, hit the road,
and make the most of the experience you painstakingly planned
for months prior.*

At least that's what I did.

I'd already faced the wedding weekend that wasn't, and though it wasn't without injury, I did make it through in one piece. So I figured I could survive our would-have-been honeymoon as well. After all, it was the last vestigial organ from my disastrous engagement. *Why not go and enjoy the ever-sunny and ever-romantic Hawaii?* I thought. I'd paid up front for our rental in Kauai, Hawaii, and since I clearly had not planned to cancel at the time I booked it, I didn't think to get trip insurance. Plus, I had never been to the remote and magical Kauai, and it had been on my bucket list for years.

Honestly, I could wax poetic about being torn or confused or unsure of what to do, but I just wasn't. To me, it was a no-brainer: it was paid for, so I was going. Hawaii or bust, baby.

Decision one was made. Now, I needed to make the far more difficult determination of who to take to paradise with me. I would assume it goes without saying, but for obvious reasons, Mr. Ex was out. Next option, please.

There was Mom, who, though she was truly a pillar of support throughout the entire ordeal, I could not quite fathom sharing both a hotel room and a bed with her once we got there. Despite my unending love for her, we both readily admit we do not share space well. She likes to stay up late, while I am an early bird. She likes it frigid, while I despise having to bundle on a tropical vacation. She falls asleep with the TV on, and it's flat out impossible for me to sleep with the tube still blaring.

You get the picture.

Then, there was The Ride or Die, who will always be my partner in crime and travel buddy. We travel spectacularly well together, but weird things constantly happen to us on our adventures–truly bizarre crap–and I wasn't sure I could handle any more snafus at the moment.

Finally, I had The Wild One, my other best friend who is always supportive and always down for an adventure. She also happened to be going through a divorce, so in terms of logistics and timing, it could not have been a more perfect time for both of us to escape.

I struggled with my choice for several weeks, until ultimately, I decided The Wild One would benefit the most from this excursion. There were only a few days remaining until our departure, so I promptly picked up the phone, gave her a ring, and delivered my sales pitch. She was immediately on board. No questions asked.

Winner, winner, chicken dinner!

Look out, Hawaii, here we come.

* * *

A few days later, as planned, I awoke, ready to leave for my very merry Un-Honeymoon, but instead of feeling my normal pre-trip excitement and euphoria, I was in the midst of the biggest funk I had suffered for a long, long time. To make matters worse, Mr. Ex chose these last few moments before my Uber arrived to pointedly text me that *"we could be married and on the way to Hawaii right now."* Like a dagger straight to my heart, he continued to say how much better that situation would be than the pit of despair we both now occupied.

Even though I disagreed we would be better off married, I was racked with gut-wrenching guilt. Twist those daggers deeper, why don't ya. I felt guilty I was still on my way to paradise. Felt guilty I was going forward with our plans despite an utter derailing of the real reason we planned to go in the first place. And ultimately, I felt guilty I'd decided to prioritize myself and regain my own happiness. I was going to a place I was hoping would bring me joy, would bring me a chance to let go of the sadness, and would potentially even allow me to relax. A place I hoped would ultimately bring me peace.

I was doing what my soul needed, but I still felt bad that it likely made him feel worse. For despite the fact that my wagon was no longer hitched to his, and logically I knew I had every right to continue on my own personal journey, I couldn't stop feeling very much in the wrong.

Arriving at the airport, dressed comfortably in a neutral maxi dress with a light scarf, open knit sweater, and my granny beach hat, of course, The Wild One and I "accidentally" ran into my mother in the airport. She said her flight just happened to arrive while we were there, but I am still convinced to this day she just wanted to check in and make sure her baby was all right. A quick hug and she bid us bon voyage.

As we taxied for takeoff, I searched for a distracting movie to put me to sleep for the entirety of the flight. I needed to sleep it all off–Mr. Ex's text, the emotions, and the guilt. Unfortunately, or perhaps fortunately, I'm still not sure, I decided to watch a movie, *On the Basis of Sex*.

This epic Ruth Bader Ginsberg biographical film features one of the strongest real life female superheroes (RBG!) I have ever seen. Most of you know her story, so I'll be quick: RBG is the definition of trusting your gut, believing in yourself and having the courage to follow through, no matter the obstacles. Point blank. Period. End of discussion.

Oh, how I longed for that level of trust in myself.

Just as the movie reached an empowering crescendo, my dear friend The Matchmaker (more on this particular moniker later) group texted me and The Wild One to reassure us both. You see, The Matchmaker is a cherished friend of ours and having gone through more than her fair share of her own personal struggles, she gives damn fine and poignant advice. It came as no surprise, then, after some general pleasantries about the irony of our current situation, that she shared this:

"To this day, I still get myself a card on March 17 (the day I left my ex and chose my happiness.) There are only great things ahead for you two and I am so excited to know such strong and beautiful women."

She closed with an appropriately light and uplifting illustration of her present-day happiness by sharing a photo of her current situation–coffee spilled all over the bathroom, her with wet hair, and a surprisingly delighted daughter giggling in the background. All of it serving as a heartfelt recognition of love and fate and timing and the hope for a better future.

Fatefully, serendipitously, whatever you choose to call it, if you add an epic heroine like RBG with The Matchmaker's text, you get the precise ingredients needed for an in-flight sob fest.

I was deeply comforted by The Matchmaker's kind words, and her hope-filled message triggered a truly gigantic release within me. I completely lost my cool and cried my heart out in the dark on a trans-Pacific flight to paradise. Sobbing like a fool, I must have looked like the craziest passenger around, but thankfully the engines were loud enough to drown out the noise. I released the remaining grief from the weeks before and I cried myself dry. Totally surrendered, I emptied my guilt into the 40,000-foot void and let the hurt float away into the atmosphere. For the first time, I let it all go for real and with finality.

Afterward, I felt more clear, more solid, and more certain of exactly who I was, what I valued, and the life I wanted and needed in the future. I was still flying through the air, but I felt grounded.

I was grounded in my beliefs, in my intuition, and in my authentic self alike.

* * *

Once we landed back on solid ground, The Wild One and I continued on in standard airport protocol. Quick pit-stop at the ladies' room to make sure I didn't look too haggard after crying all flight: check. Secure the overstuffed luggage of ladies who always overpack: check. Pick up the rental car...oops.

We schlepped up to read the digital ticker board upon our arrival at the Hertz carousel and located my name.

Your CHEVROLET CAMARO CV SS is parked in STALL 880.

FML.

As a wedding surprise for Mr. Ex, I'd reserved a brand new, cherry red Chevrolet Camaro SS. I was trying to be thoughtful, and it was our honeymoon, after all, so I'd decided to splurge. The only problem was after confirming said rental six months prior, I forgot what I'd rented. Such is the life of an advanced planner.

Walking to the car with our luggage in tow, I was irritated at myself for giving in to such frivolity as I was now genuinely worried that a) our luggage would never fit, and b) I would be thinking about Mr. Ex even more as I drove this bright red sports car around the island. I wanted to release. I wanted to move forward. Now I had to sit in a flaming hot reminder of my failure once again?

I could feel the old whispers of guilt trying to regain their hold in my head. I could feel the negative emotions trying to reinhabit the void they'd vacated only hours before. I could feel the pull of all the mess I was trying so desperately to leave behind, like a weight trying to pull me down to the depths of the ocean.

I could feel it all, and then...

I pressed the gas on the first straightaway and effortlessly accelerated from zero to sixty in what I swear was two seconds flat. It felt like we were only driving twenty mph and yet, The Wild One and I were cruising along at warp speed from even the tiniest of taps on the gas.

As we flew down the highway, the weight evaporated. The negative emotions floated away once more and instead of sadness, I felt empowered, excited, and joyous. I remembered how grateful I should be to even have the opportunity to drive this car. I remembered the encouraging text from The Matchmaker. I remembered the badassery of RBG. I remembered the grace I promised to give myself and the space I was allowed to heal. I remembered my freedom and the potential futures I could now explore. I remembered my own strength, and I felt said energy reflected back at me in the horsepower contained under my right foot.

The car felt like it wanted to be driven more, driven faster, right to the edge of its full potential. It wanted to up and go, unencumbered by anyone or anything. It longed to be free, and so did I. The car and I, we were one wild, free, joyous being, cruising together down the heavenly highways of Hawaii.

What could be better than that?

* * *

The Wild One and I pulled up to our rental and I was immediately grateful to have her by my side as I promptly had to explain to the cute gentleman who was there to give us our key why my husband was not going to be joining us. Ever. To say this was an awkward exchange is a gross understatement. Although, yes, it wasn't so uncomfortable I couldn't notice how stinking cute this guy was. I was newly un-engaged, not dead!

With no real plans, other than pure relaxation and wellness, The Wild One and I easily settled into a perfect daily routine. We awoke early each day, made delicious Kona coffee, and began our sunrise reflections, yoga sessions, and a short abdominal workout series. (I'm one of those weirdos who genuinely enjoys working out on vacation).

We then checked our emails, did work for just long enough to make us feel like we deserved to take a break, and dove headfirst into the cool bliss of the pool. We drank kombucha, cooked fresh, healthy meals, and soaked up the rays, convinced they were rapidly recharging our personal batteries.

Once 5:00 p.m. rolled around, we sipped one perfectly chilled glass of French rosé as we danced around the living room to our hearts' content, supremely happy and in awe of the natural beauty surrounding us.

I guess you could say we were fully committed to the Luke Bryan program–"Sunrise, Sunburn, Sunset," repeat–and I wasn't complaining.

I did plan an extra special excursion, which forced us to break from our everyday rhythm–one of my favorite beachfront pastimes of all time, surfing!

As odd as it sounds, given the fact that I am originally from landlocked Oklahoma and currently live in Colorado, I have always considered myself a surfer girl. In high school, I wore Billabong this and Pac Sun that. I swear, just ask The Ride or Die, who lightheartedly made fun of me for this phase just the other day. I tooled around in my forest green SUV, windows down, wearing a bikini top and board shorts like I was either heading to or coming from the Oklahoma beaches. I pretty much thought I was the long-lost character from *Blue Crush*.

As an adult, I still wear Billabong and not so secretly think of myself as a Cali Girl at heart. Even as I drafted this chapter, I laughed out loud realizing I was wearing a Cal State Long Beach cut-off tank top, both as a shout out to my old volleyball days, and as a way to feel closer to the beach in even the smallest way possible. I concede I sometimes also secretly hope people think I'm actually from SoCal (slaps palm to head in shame). Anyhow, I share all this to illustrate just how pumped I was to get back out on the water. Back to the salty, yummy, powerful, beautiful expanse of the sea.

Despite my love of surf culture, I did hire an instructor in acknowledgment of my still very much novice ability actually catching waves.

Mr. Surf Sensei rolled up in the classic surf-bum vehicle of a salt-covered red Jeep with surfboards galore bungeed to the roof. Long, gray, wavy hair blowing in the wind, he walked up the drive and deposited his already wet and sandy flip flops at the door. He was warm and sturdy and genuine as he shook our hands, but he was also slightly confused.

Once again, I had to answer questions about why Mr. Ex was not on our honeymoon, but to his credit, Mr. Surf Sensei wasn't fazed in the slightest. He immediately exclaimed, "His loss, our gain" and waved his arm in a "follow me" motion as The Wild One and I scrambled to grab our things and follow him promptly out the door. So much for slowly easing into it!

Once on the beach, I put on my rash guard and latched my ankle strap firmly to my leg, standing tall and ready, like a gladiator about to head into battle. We went through the standard introduction about paddling out, safety, and proper form, and then we mentally and physically prepared for the task at hand.

We wanted to enjoy ourselves, sure, but we also wanted to be good! At least I did.

"Just relax and have some fun, will ya!" said Mr. Surf Sensei, as he immediately pegged me as a perfectionist, which to be fair, I am. He clearly knew he had his work cut out for him.

Determined to succeed, I paddled out with gusto. I lined up properly, started out in a good spot on the wave, and then for some unknown reason, I got scared. I started to pop up, and before I even had the chance to lose my balance, I immediately bailed off my board.

What a flipping disaster.

I was supremely annoyed at myself for jumping ship so quickly and cursed the surf gods for not helping me effortlessly remaster the art of surfing as I so expected I would.

Womp, womp, womp.

Paddling out harder this time, my second attempt was a bit better, but still lackluster overall.

Then the third was worse.

"What is happening?!" I muttered to no one in particular, smacking the surface of the water with my palm.

No doubt recognizing my rapidly impending shame spiral, Mr. Surf Sensei paddled over and pulled up to sit on his board next to me as we bobbed in the waves.

"How's it goin', kid?" he asked.

"Ugh, I don't know why I'm so bad!" I exclaimed. "I do actually know how to surf," I reassured him weakly, "but I'm totally in my head." Two points for self-awareness.

"You gotta get out of there, kid," he chuckled. "You're getting in your own way."

I mean, it wasn't quite the "Do Less" mantra of Paul Rudd's Kunu character in *Forgetting Sarah Marshall*, but it was pretty darn close.

"You're strong. You know you're strong. Just trust your body to do what it knows how to do," he continued.

"What if I can't?" I asked.

"I promise you, you can. Trust yourself."

Little did he know how sound his advice was at this particular juncture in my life. I knew I needed to trust myself in life, and now I needed to prove I could do it by trusting myself in surfing.

Game on.

"I got this!" I said resolutely under my breath.

Finally, it clicked. I let go of the all-consuming drive for perfection and simply trusted my body to do what it has done hundreds of times before. I got out of my head and focused on enjoying the moment for the undeniable blessing it was. A blessing of laughing, learning to surf, and floating unencumbered in the wide, vast sea.

I totally let go, and by doing so, I found the elusive liquid balance required when surfing. Unsteady and solid at the same time, I flowed, and it felt so darn good to be back in my body.

Wave after wave, I got up, rode the crest, dropped in on a dime, and soared across the smooth face of the wave. I'd bail on purpose this time, and then burst through the frothy surface with a huge smile lighting up my face. Laughing, I'd hop on and do it again. It was exhausting and exhilarating all at once.

Dog-tired but cheerfully weary, I paused to take it all in. I rotated my board away from the beach and set the nose toward the horizon. I sat up tall, reached my palms out wide by my side, and egg-beatered my legs slowly while I closed my eyes and turned my face up to greet the sun.

Seeing me stop, Mr. Surf Sensei came over to check if I was all right.

"Don't worry, I'm just taking in the moment." I said calmly without even opening my eyes.

"Gotcha, kid." His voice sounded like he smiled back in clear recognition of the inner peace I was feeling, and he paddled away silently to work with The Wild One.

No more words were needed. He got it.

He understood I am never as relaxed as when I am floating, swimming, or surfing in a body of saltwater. To me, the ocean is cleansing, supportive, and flows with an utterly natural rhythm.

Laying back, the noises faded away, and my thoughts drifted naturally to hopefulness as the sun bathed me in positive, energizing light. Truly, heaven is rocking slowly in the sun-kissed, salty waves. Even now, I can close my eyes and feel these moments with such great intensity and near physical sensation that it almost brings me to tears with gratitude.

Sadly, though, all moments, however divine, are ultimately fleeting, and after what felt like only an instant, our lesson was over. Four hours of paddling and surfing and falling later, I was physically exhausted. But in place of the turmoil and doubt of the last several months, I was emotionally calm and even newly confident in myself and the direction of my life. I had exorcized the demons right out of me, and like my crying purge on the plane, I was left an empty vessel. A vessel the sea could now refill and rebuild with waves of happiness, strength, and trust in oneself.

I walked out of the water, shook out my hair, and felt invincible. I'm not entirely sure how, but I knew I could finally hold onto this confidence for the months and years ahead. I knew I could trust my authentic self and I knew I could just be me.

Just me, and it would be enough.

Like I said, it's amazing what a little time on a board can do for the mind.

And just in case I was tempted to forget my newfound inner peace, our surf outing also left me with a gentle physical reminder as well. Since I forgot to sunscreen my hands, I consequently looked like I was wearing weirdly red, sunburned dinner gloves for several days to follow.

Cool.

Chapter 15

Closure

"Every story has an end. But in life,
every ending is just a new beginning."

– Uptown Girls

Wedding Countdown: Two months after
A few months had passed since our June non-wedding, and I finally thought I had moved on–well, at least moved forward a little bit. Every piece of my mess had been handled, managed, signed, sealed, delivered, or destroyed. Mr. Ex and I didn't have closure per se, but we felt more resolved and content in our now separate paths. Heck, we were both dating again, but more on that later. Time to wrap the unwedding, the unplanning–hell, the entire relationship–with a pretty pale pink bow and put it to bed forever.

Or so I thought. It seems the universe had one last gut-punch, just for good measure.

One afternoon in early August, I got a call from my all-time favorite framers. I picked up excitedly, as I was midway through framing some new local art, and I was hopeful one of the pieces was ready for pickup.

Mr. Owner was on the other line, and we exchanged a few pleasantries before he tentatively asked, "Is your mother in town?" Though at first glance this may seem odd, it's actually not an entirely peculiar question, since I'd referred my mom to the shop. Still, Mr. Owner seemed disproportionately nervous for an as yet unknown reason.

"Sadly, no, she's in Oklahoma right now," I replied lightly.

"Well, she has a piece at the store that's been here for several months. I hate to ask this but is there any way you would be able to come pick it up for her?" he asked.

"Of course!" I said, also not surprised since I had been her personal delivery service many times before. "I'll be by in half an hour."

That afternoon, I popped buoyantly into the store. They brought out the tightly wrapped art from the back, but I couldn't resist the urge to ask what she had framed.

"What is it this time?" I asked like a little kid at Christmas trying desperately not to peek at the presents under the tree.

"Ummm," Mr. Owner stalled. "I think it was your wedding guestbook."

"Ohhh, I see," I managed as my smile waned, remembering how Mr. Ex and I had commissioned a watercolor portrait of one of our engagement photos, around which we had planned for our friends and family to sign the matting.

"I wrapped it up, though, so you don't have to see it," he added apologetically.

"That's OK," I said, knowing full well it wasn't his fault and desperately trying not to make him feel even worse than he clearly already did.

When he still looked sad, I added a bit overenthusiastically, "I promise! I'm fine!" Note to self, blurting out "I'm fine" makes you seem anything but.

Stomach momentarily in my shoes, I carried my sad little package to the car, promptly dropped it at Mom's, and wanted nothing more than to shake it all off. It had been so long since an emotional shockwave had gone through me like this, but I wasn't all sad this time. I mean, sure, it brought heartache, but grief wasn't what stuck out most.

Nope.

This time I was completely and totally exasperated. I was very much over riding the emotional rollercoaster of the past few months, and I just wanted to get off the bloody ride already. I wanted closure. I wanted to move on. I wanted to be done.

So, that was it. Our guestbook was the final straw.

Had my experience been painful? Sure. Scary? Hell yea. But I made it!

I was not only officially on the other side, but I was living, people! I was ready to live for me again and all I needed to do was give myself permission.

Yup, I thought, *let's close this chapter, shall we?*

Or, in the infamous words of Lizzo, it's "About Damn Time."

* * *

Fortuitously, Mr. Ex and I were scheduled to meet for coffee just a few days later. We planned to meet at a Starbucks equidistant between where he was now living in south Denver and our former home in the Highlands, a halfway coffee house, I guess you could call it. We had a few last knick-knacks to exchange, but in all honesty, those were just an excuse to see each other one last time.

You see, as time slowly slipped by and days turned into weeks, and weeks crept into months so, too, did a feeling of nostalgia creep in.

No longer was I in utter anguish when I thought about our failed relationship and the future we would never have.

No longer was I angry.

No longer did I feel shame or hurt.

No longer did I focus so intently on why we were wrong for each other in every way imaginable.

I had healed the giant Mr. Ex-sized hole in my heart and healed the grief of what we lost when I walked away. Piece by piece, I had built myself back into a person I loved and cherished. And through my healing and quieting and listening and rebuilding, I was able to love and cherish the best parts of Mr. Ex again as well, just in a new way.

Time had washed away the sting of our uncoupling and only the highlight reel of our life together remained upon the shore of my mind: wearing silly matching animal onesies, just for the heck of it. Waking up at dawn to hike across the lava fields in Hawaii Volcanoes National Park. Derby Days and kickball teams and theme parties and too many sporting events to recount. Trips to Cape San Blas, where we played football in the waves, snorkeled in search of fresh bay scallops for dinner, walked along the beaches at sunset, and lounged in the sun as the salty air fed our souls as much as the baked oysters fed our hungry bellies. Exploring Costa Rica then lounging outside the literal shack we happily called home for the week. The laughs we shared as we danced ridiculously in bars, in clubs, in our kitchen, wherever the mood struck and without regard for who was watching. The goofiness, the fun, the love. So many happy memories remained, untarnished and untouched by the flames of our demise.

I was able to celebrate it all and I realized how much I genuinely valued those bits of Mr. Ex I fell in love with in the first place. His sense of humor, his protectiveness, his coy smile hiding the mischievous nature at his core, his confidence, his dedication to a costume, his ability to make me feel like the only woman in the room.

As I pulled into the parking lot, a fleeting thought passed through my mind, *Could we get back together after all?* followed quickly by, *Is it natural to wonder what if? Maybe we can make it work. Or maybe this is exactly what we both need to finally move on for real this time. Maybe it's OK to cherish the memories for what they are, memories. Maybe the past is where they should stay.*

I waffled back and forth, uncertain as to how this coffee would play out and also unsure of the Mr. Ex I was about to meet.

Would I receive a warm welcome like the almond milk latte at kids' temperature I typically order, or would he ice me out completely like a cold brew pouring through the room?

No more stalling, it was time to find out.

In a somewhat uncharacteristic move on his part, Mr. Ex was early. He sat at a table on the far side of the room illuminated by the soft morning sun shining through the floor-to-ceiling windows behind him, backlighting him like an angelic vision. *Glad to see he's still so drop-dead gorgeous*, I thought to myself with a smile.

He raised that chiseled jaw as I approached his table, and our eyes locked for the first time in what felt like an eternity. Like seas of blue, I thought I might drown in the depth of those familiar eyes right then and there.

To my surprise, he smiled a warm and reassuring and hopeful smile. I exhaled the breath I didn't even realize I had been holding and smiled back with genuine relief. He stood and put his arm around me in an awkward side hug, which I returned with equal unease. To break the ice, we got our iced coffees and settled back into the booth.

We talked about exactly what you would expect from two people who used to be engaged but now acted more like acquaintances: How's work? How's your mom? And your grandparents? Do you like your new apartment? Have you seen any of our friends lately? Do you hate me for ruining your life? You know, normal stuff.

The funny thing was it was shockingly easy. Awkward, for sure, but also comforting. We were able to laugh our way through over an hour of pleasant conversation, and as our time together crept to an end once again, I think we both wished it were longer. There were obviously still so many unresolved issues and grief between us, but above it all, there was hope. Hope for us both!

There was a realization that somehow, we had made it through this trauma together and had emerged battered but better people for it. We were no longer lovers, but we could honor the love we once shared, setting each other free to find what was truly meant to be. How empowering and incredible and mature is that, y'all!

One last glance over the tops of our cups and it was finally time to say goodbye for good. Knowing there would be tears involved on both sides and not wanting to make a scene at Starbucks so early in the morning, we walked outside to the parking lot for our final farewell.

Standing next to his big, black, classic Georgia-boy truck, Mr. Ex wrapped those long, athletic, familiar arms of his 6′4″ frame around me, enveloping my entire body in his. The essence of him coming off in waves and his smell, oh man, his smell.

It's said that scent has the power to summon a lifetime of memories in an instant. Breathing in the unique blend of his personal perfume, our entire relationship seemed to flash before my eyes, like a movie played at five times the speed.

The good, the bad, the ugly—it all washed over me like a wave of sensation as I lingered in his arms. Tears slowly began to roll down my face as I tried to savor this last hug, storing the warmth, the feeling, the fragrance, and the former love in my memories forever.

This is how I wanted to remember us. Maybe we weren't happy together, but maybe we could happily wish each other well apart.

One last hug as a parting gift, as a true goodbye, and as a moment of closure for us both. For that, I am forever grateful.

* * *

Wedding Countdown: Three years after

For the longest time, I wondered what it would be like if we ever saw each other again. I mean, Denver is a small town and the potential for an unplanned run-in wasn't totally out of the question.

Would we cross paths in LoDo, perhaps at a Rockies baseball game where Mr. Ex still frequented outings with his buddies? Would we accidentally bump our shopping carts together at the ever-popular Whole Foods in Cherry Creek, subsequently exchanging pleasantries over carts filled with the week's provisions? Would we attend the wedding of a mutual friend and be forced to watch a major life milestone we had planned to do together?

Would it be awkward and tense? Would it cause a swell of unresolved feelings I thought were long gone? Would the air once again fill with sadness? Or would it be bittersweet?

Instead of pain, would there be healing? Would we look upon one another with fondness and nostalgic mutual respect? Could there even be joy, or was that hoping for too much?

Though I had romantically moved on in every way possible, I still thought of this potential interaction often. And yet it wasn't until three years later we finally crossed paths.

As fate would have it, mere days after I got engaged to my now husband in Burgundy, France, of all places (sorry, spoiler alert!), I received an email from Mr. Ex himself. You better believe my stomach dropped like a rock, but I was intrigued, nonetheless.

The subject line read, "Truck Title."

Upon reading the body of the email, it turned out that although Mr. Ex was supposed to remove my name from the title of his truck when we broke up three years prior, despite his assurances he had done it all properly, somehow the paperwork was never successfully filed. As a result, my name was still on the title, and he couldn't sell said truck without a signature from yours truly.

This was most certainly not how I expected our first real meeting to occur post-breakup, but my options were to a) wait to receive the paperwork from Mr. Ex in the mail, then print, sign, and mail the forms back to Mr. Ex or b) meet him at a CarMax in North Denver to sign the paperwork in person. I was living between Denver and London, England, at the time and was set to fly back to the United Kingdom two days later (a story for another day), so my only option was to bite the bullet and head north for our meet up. We exchanged pleasant emails filled with "hope you are wells" and other well wishes as we coordinated the time and place. The stage was set. Tomorrow at 11:00 a.m., you, me, a black F-150, and a whole lot of history.

Through mutual friends, I was aware Mr. Ex had recently gotten engaged and welcomed a precious new baby girl with his fiancée, but I wasn't sure if he had yet received the news of my own engagement. I was trepidatious, but I hoped since I was so genuinely thrilled for the recent blessings in his life, maybe he could return the sentiment. I also wanted to look my absolute best, as is only natural, in my opinion. I hoped to look at least as good as when we were together, if not better, so I dressed in my best casual but chic ensemble. Mr. Ex clearly wanted to prove the same as we were both dressed well above what Emily Post would consider appropriate for a casual day at the dealership.

My anxiety was fully sky high as I drove north on I-25 to meet my former partner.

Nervous sweats, check.

Racing heart, check.

Stomach clenched in a million tiny knots, check.

I was so completely and totally on edge to see the man I once loved, the man I once agreed to marry. Not because I was worried about anything in particular, mind you, but because I so wholeheartedly wanted us to have a positive interaction that would let me know we were both doing great. Maybe even an interaction that would show me Mr. Ex was thriving, and in a way, reinforce I had made the right decision for him, as much I had for me. A girl can dream, right?

I pulled into the parking lot, remembering the last time I was about to meet Mr. Ex in Starbucks so many years before. I willed my nerves to calm and tried to reassure my body that the fight-or-flight response I was currently battling was totally overkill.

"Let's get this show on the road," I said as I climbed out into the sun.

Walking in, I was a bit disoriented at first, unsure what desk out of the twenty or so scattered about the massive showroom was the one I was meant to find. Then, I heard his deep, southern drawl, call out to me, "Katherine, over here."

I turned to see the man I almost married walking toward me with what can only be described as confidence, dripping with his signature Mr. Ex swagger. I was glad to see at least some things never change! Crossing the gap between us in only a few strides, we were soon face to face.

"How are ya?" he twanged. "Did you find it all right?"

"Oh yeah, no problems at all. How are you?!" I answered with a bit too much nervous enthusiasm.

"I'm just fine. Let's get this done so you can be on your way," he said as I followed his lead toward the lounge where we would wait to sign away our last piece of joint property.

We were informed it would likely take about an hour for the final inspection, only after which would I be able to sign over the title for sale, so we settled into the lounge and finally let out a joint sigh. We had seen each other. There was no spontaneous combustion, no arguments, no issues, no fights–really no negativity at all. We just looked at each other and started laughing in mutual amusement and wonder at how we'd ended up here.

"So, tell me all the things!" I said, knowing of at least two exciting developments in his world.

"Well, I'm guessing you know that I recently got engaged?" he began.

"I do," I confirmed with a smile.

"And we just had a baby girl!" he added, his blue eyes sparkling with pride.

"The Blonde One told me! I'm so thrilled for you, Mr. Ex," I replied warmly.

"And I hear congratulations are in order for you as well? Plus, I see an engagement ring, so the rumors must be true," he continued, sneaking a quick peek at my bejeweled ring finger.

"They are. It literally happened two weeks ago, so we haven't planned anything yet, but we're excited."

"I bet. I'm so glad to hear it," he said genuinely.

Hottest of topics out of the way, we continued our deep dive, getting to re-know you chat for over an hour. He talked about his sweet baby and the way her thick, full hair stuck up all over the place, just as Mr. Ex's had when he was a wee one. He confirmed with photo evidence. He told me about his fiancée, and how they met, and what she did for work, and where they were living, and what they were thinking for the wedding. We talked about his job, and his preparation to transition to the role of stay-at-home dad, which was something he'd always wanted to do, but which was fundamentally in opposition to me wanting to stay home with the kids, save for this book, of course! We shared stories of our families, as I loved his family as much as he loved mine. I told him how I met my own newly minted fiancé, and what was going on with work, and why I was currently living in the UK, and how my precious Doberman, Gucci, was doing. Basically, we shared the story of the lives we built apart as we simultaneously recounted endless memories of our shared lives, focusing fully on the joy and love of our season together.

We laughed in the way two people with a deeply intertwined history can, but in a completely untangled and undramatic way. We were at peace in our own worlds, and this allowed us to remain at peace together. In fact, I don't think I had ever seen Mr. Ex happier or more relaxed. Father and husband-to-be to someone who wasn't me clearly worked for him!

Things were going so well I was almost disappointed when Mr. CarMax finally called us over to sign the papers and told us we could be on our way. Little did he know how true his statement rang!

Officially uncoupled in every way, Mr. Ex walked me outside to my car this time. We stood there for a moment, unsure how to end things in a way that was respectful to each other, respectful to our current partners, and somehow also reverential of what we once shared.

I'm awkward, so I extended my hand with a weird, "Welp, it was good to see you?" as my voice questioningly raised at the end of what should have been a declarative sentence.

Once more, he laughed, and as he put one arm around my shoulders for a non-intimate side hug, he said something I never thought I'd hear, "Thank you."

"You're welcome," I returned, as I platonically side-squeezed him back.

With that, Mr. Ex turned and walked back out of my life, and back toward the true future he was always meant to have.

Climbing into my car, I smiled with deep relief and a freeing breath I felt like I had been holding since the very day I said yes in Champagne. We had officially made it through. Through the CarMax meetup, through the healing, through the breakup, through the torture we put each other through for months prior, through the grief, the pain, and the guilt. We had made it through the fire, and we had finally arrived on the other side.

Still, as I drove home to my true forever person, I couldn't help but shake the feeling that his thank you was somehow more meaningful than I originally gave it credit. Yes, he was thanking me for meeting him to sort out the truck situation. But in my heart, I also felt like perhaps he was thanking me for the life situation as well, for being brave enough to make a decision that ultimately served us both, for trusting my intuition, and for freeing us both to pursue a truly meant to be love. A thank you for leading us both to the infinitely happier lives we were now living.

Subconsciously, or maybe even consciously, I believe he was reinforcing what I knew all along…

What was not meant for me, was not meant for him, either.

Thank the Lord I trusted myself enough for the both of us.

Part III
Ever After

"And while Cinderella and her prince did live happily
ever after, the point, gentlemen, is that they lived."
– *Ever After: A Cinderella Story*

KATHERINE ROSE WOLLER

Chapter 16

Re-Entry

"Sometimes, you have to step outside of the person you've
been and remember the person you were meant to be.
The person you want to be. The person you are."
– H.G. Wells

Wedding Countdown: One week after
To those of you looking for guidance on when it
is acceptable to re-enter the dating world, I do not have one
definitive, quantitative answer for you. Frankly, I think you
have probably realized you will not find a "one size fits all"
description of any specific guidance in this book, nor will
you find an adequate answer via various online queries that
direct you to the few and far between blog posts that cover
"what to do when you call off your wedding."

Trust me on this one.

Now, if you're like me, when I began considering my
reentry into the dating world, I was looking for a solid
benchmark, an actual number on when it was "OK" to date.
Unfortunately, not a single source produced a firm number
and most repeatedly stuck by the vague guidance that there
is no set timeline for when it is advisable to open your heart
to someone new.

Ever the rule follower, I wanted a hard and fast rule to confirm my projected timeline, dang it.

Perhaps my various searches were too specific for Google?

Perhaps people were keeping this secret number to themselves?

Or perhaps, as an AI query last week confirmed, there was no one right answer.

I lean heavily toward the latter.

Even still, I needed something, anything really to make me feel better. Any way to understand when I was allowed to start putting my love life back together. More specifically, I wanted to clarify whether or not I, as the wedding-calling-off-er, needed to wait for the jilted Mr. Ex to go on his own first post-engagement date before I tested the waters myself. It just felt wrong to date before Mr. Ex dated, and I was afraid to hurt everyone even more than I already had.

I was still grappling with this dilemma, as well as the destroyed remains of life as I knew it, when, for better or for worse, I discovered I didn't have to wait any longer to date after all. For Mr. Ex was promptly back on the dating apps in all his Glen Powell glory.

How did I know this, you ask?

Like any proper girl network in a town the size of Denver, my friends had friends of friends of friends who had already matched with him, taken screenshots of each and every photo he was using on his profile, and made sure to have the date and timestamp included so there was no disputing the irrefutable evidence that he was, in fact, moving on. Now, I'm not entirely sure this level of detail was necessary, or helpful quite frankly, but that's beside the point. Pay no attention to the fact that I was still completely and totally broken from the inside out; theoretically, I was cleared for take-off.

In short, though I was well aware I still had more growth, more learning, and more self-love to cultivate, it seemed the universe wanted me to do so through a few more "failed" relationships.

One of my first new potential suitors appeared mere days after I discovered Mr. Ex's Tinder, when I was asked out via Instagram DM. As you can probably ascertain from his mode of contact, he was a young one. A twenty-two-year-old major league soccer player, to be exact. Now, I love what the Brits call a "footballer," but my first thought was...

ARE YOU KIDDING ME?

This was the dating pool in which I was now required to flail about wildly trying to find a suitable mate my age? Had I been out of the game so long that DM propositions were actually the new normal and acceptable dating prequel? Perhaps for a booty call, sure, but an actual date with a qualified candidate? I certainly hoped not.

In all honesty, though, after the initial shock and horror subsided, my second thought was a momentary consideration that perhaps it *wooouuuulllld* be kinda fun. Now, I can admit I was deeply flattered. It felt nice to be desired by the eight-pack-wielding Mr. Footballer, because damn, he was hot! But Adonis-like looks aside, Mr. Footballer wasn't going to be my first foray back into dating, so I won't take up any more page space with his particular overture.

Soon after, though, I did decide to start dating more age-appropriate candidates. I figured if Mr. Ex thought he was ready, perhaps I was ready, too. Never mind the facts that mere weeks had passed since calling off the engagement, I still had no idea what I wanted in life, and I was still sorting out who the hell I actually was.

Dating couldn't hurt, could it?

In her autobiography, *Open Book: A Memoir,* Jessica Simpson wrote that when she left Nick Lachey after having a deep, emotional connection with Johnny Knoxville, she wasn't escaping her marriage to be with anyone else. She was escaping to be with herself.

Read that again: *She was escaping to be with herself.*

Never have her words rang truer, for that is exactly what I did when I left Mr. Ex. I escaped my engagement to be with my authentic self.

Not Mr. Footballer.

Not some random on a dating app.

I left for me. Just me.

And that was enough.

Once freed, though, the unending support from Mr. New Orleans–yes, the Mr. New Orleans from Chapter 5– resulted in my curiosity finally getting the best of me. Over the past two months, we had developed a real friendship and there was no denying he was my trusted confidant.

So, a few weeks after calling it off with Mr. Ex, Mr. New Orleans and I decided to give it a go. Even typing those words, I grimace at how quick it sounds, but I was trying to move forward with my life, ready and healed or not.

I'd like to think it was only natural I would consider the "what if" of giving Mr. New Orleans a shot. After all, how could I feel such an instant and deep connection with this stranger? *Surely it must mean something,* I thought.

A friendship turned romantic, it's what we are all supposed to want, right?

So, whether it was smart or not, we planned to meet up in Chicago and see if the connection was still there.

I was visiting The Single Lady, and since she had introduced us all in the first place, we were going to pursue a proper group hang, complete with Sunday brunches and Cubs games at Wrigley Field! Since this plan combined two of my absolute favorite things, baseball and brunch, I was already pumped beyond belief. Add the opportunity to explore my bond with Mr. New Orleans, and I was ready for a weekend of Chicago summer fun.

I won't lie, it felt so stinking nice. Easy, playful, joyous, it was the perfect painkiller for my life of self-inflicted torment back home. Mr. New Orleans himself was the ideal antidote to bring me out of my perpetual funk and awaken me to the world like Sleeping Beauty as she gloriously reanimates post finger prick. Like Prince Phillip, he helped bring me back to life with a single weekend of friends and fun.

Our little foursome, The Single Lady, Mr. New Orleans, his bestie, and I, did it all. We walked along the riverfront, laughing and soaking up the warm summer sun. We brunched outside on a patio in River North, sipping salty Bloody Mary's and indulging guiltlessly in eggs benedict galore. We window shopped the designer storefronts of the infamous Viagra Triangle and ogled the sexy mid-life-crisis sports cars that revved as they sped past. We visited the Chicago 2016 Cubs World Series Trophy, strolled through Wrigleyville, cheered unabashedly for the Cubs at the top of our lungs, and even hit up the batting cages in the bar after the game where I showed off my former Varsity Softball skills.

We let our inner children run wild and let me tell you, it was glorious. I was finally living for ME again.

It also didn't hurt that our slow-burn chemistry translated really dang well, if you know what I mean.

* * *

A few weeks later, Mr. New Orleans made the trek to me this time and flew in for a quick weekend in Denver. I wanted to show him Colorado's finest, and my finest, as well, as we sought to see what time spent with just us two would feel like. As with any guest who is not from the mountains, I decided to take him hiking and exploring to show him the natural beauty of the state I love so much. After all, I needed to suss out not only if he felt the same but also determine if he could keep up! I'm a wanderer at heart, and I needed to know from the jump if Mr. New Orleans could hack it.

We spent the first morning hiking Herman Gulch (which is stunning in any season), and then made the short but gorgeous drive to grab lunch in Breckenridge, spending the afternoon strolling the picturesque alpine streets with no particular agenda other than enjoyment. Yet, as we walked down Main Street, I couldn't shake the nagging feeling I didn't actually want to be there.

You see, I used to ski in Breckenridge with Mr. Ex, and every corner seemed to hold a memory that still haunted me, letting me know I was nowhere near healed. However, where I was able to be completely honest with Mr. New Orleans before, I no longer felt the same ability to speak my truth. I mean, how do you tell a man who just flew across the country for you that you're still struggling with feelings for your ex-fiancé?

True, he theoretically knew what he was signing up for, but it's one thing to know someone is going through the phases of breakup; it's quite another for those phases to slap you in the face at every turn of the trail.

The reality was in the hot, harsh light of the Colorado summer sun, maybe things weren't as healed and carefree and easy as they'd originally seemed.

I couldn't relax and enjoy knowing some very real part of me was still hurting and likely some very real part of Mr. Ex would be hurt as well if he saw me here with Mr. New Orleans. Tinder profile be damned. It was too much, too soon.

Only ten minutes into our exploration of town, I asked Mr. New Orleans if we could head home. I'm pretty sure I made up some lame excuse about tummy troubles, which was believable, as I have battled gastrointestinal distress for years, but was in that moment a bold-faced lie. It wasn't a pain of the gut, it was a pain of the heart, and I needed relief. I hoped getting out of Breck would get us back on track and allow me to find joy in his companionship once more. Funnily enough, I did have a sudden attack of the poops on the drive home, so I guess karma really got a good laugh out of that one.

Back in the city, I needed space. I needed air. I needed time to think and a place to emotionally process. I needed the safe haven of my worn leather couch, a cup of Earl Grey, and maybe even a Hallmark movie or two. More importantly, though, I needed to be with me and me alone. Unfortunately for us both, Mr. New Orleans was staying with me.

When he first said he wanted to stay together, I felt uneasy about having another man in the house Mr. Ex and I had previously called home. I knew it would make me uncomfortable, and, quite frankly, sad, but I chose to push back the unprocessed grief in an attempt to move forward, albeit prematurely. I was the one who had said yes to this arrangement, and I was to blame for the regret now running through me.

Mr. New Orleans was perceptive enough to sense I needed a break, so he offered to go for a run while I settled in and settled down. How he still had the energy to run after the day we'd had, I will never know, but I digress.

While he was out, I stripped off the sweaty, sticky clothes of the day and hoped I could chuck my bad mood in the hamper along with them. I soaked endlessly in the hot, steamy shower, attempting to suds away the anxiety creeping up my spine. I let the water scald my skin in an almost self-injurious effort to feel something else, anything else but grief.

Damp, I emerged from the shower, wiped the steam from my mirror and gazed at the girl looking back. Make-up free, I could see the dark circles enshrining her eyes, the downturned corners of her mouth, and the longing for more still seeping from every pore.

I need to be alone. I need my space. This doesn't feel right. Not this! I heard my intuition whisper back at my reflection. The familiar refrain returned with ferocity as I suddenly felt the need to flee.

I genuinely do not remember how the next day of the trip went, for all I recall is thinking, *When will this be over?* I remember wishing away our time together and counting down the minutes until Mr. New Orleans would board a plane bound back to his own home. I remember being cold and pulling back, and I remember he seemed hurt by my actions. I remember I didn't care, for in those moments, selfishly, all I had the capacity to focus on was me. Nothing more, nothing less. Looking back, the whole of the Colorado trip really was the nail in the proverbial coffin of our new relationship.

Ever the optimist, though, I went to see Mr. New Orleans one last time in a hopeful effort to salvage things. I was determined to enjoy a more positive weekend of one-on-one time, and I genuinely gave it the old college try. Whether it was his nature, or the way in which we met, or the will of the fates once again, I will never know, but for some reason it was all so serious. It was all so heavy, so meaningful.

He held my hand and talked excitedly about our future. Of romantic getaways, of potential future homes together and the towns we could build a life in, of engagement ring styles and where to source them. He talked of kiddos and life goals and "maybe one days" he seemed to want tomorrow. He said all the things a woman in a serious relationship wants to hear, but we weren't in a serious relationship yet! What once brought me back to life was now consuming my life in a way that gave me shivers, like a deep, bone-chilling wind in December. It was still early fall, but I was already pulling back into my den for the winter.

Then, as he drove me to the airport, things solidified once and for all. The carefree distractions of our weekends had passed, and a more somber air permeated the car. It was no longer a cinematic dream, it was real. And what's worse,

Mr. New Orleans had made it clear he was expecting it to get realer, and fast.

In reaction to the weight of the situation, I felt the final shift within like the click of a pin in a lock on a safe. It was small at first, but as the miles ticked by on our drive to the airport, the feeling grew into a gigantic lump in my throat I could neither swallow, nor ignore.

What the hell am I doing? I thought. *I'm not ready for this, not ready for more, not ready for anyone but myself.*

Nope. Nope. Nope.

Riding silently in his car, I knew then it was already over for me. It was too dang much and too dang soon, and once again, I needed out. Yet, when the moment came, I couldn't or wouldn't articulate my honest feelings and tell him my newfound realization. So, we kissed goodbye. Me knowing it was a forever farewell, and him thinking it was just the beginning. I boarded my plane back to reality and the rapid and turbulent demise of Mr. New Orleans and me commenced.

Reflecting on this time, which I have done over and over and over again, I realize I didn't even consciously register what was happening until it was too late. It flat out didn't occur to me I was leading him on. After all, it felt too gloriously and deliciously good to smile again. That is, until it didn't. Understandably, he wanted more than I was willing to give, and the tension was palpable. He was pulling with all his might, while I was pushing away with equal force. I was taking my life one day at a time, one step at a time, once second at a time even, and I was terrified of falling back into a pattern of being someone else's version of perfect and therefore the exact same kind of prison I had just escaped. I felt myself boarding the same kind of runaway train, the same load of expectations, the same inauthentic future and pressures to perform. Sure, Mr. New Orleans might have been able to actually see and understand the real me, but I was scared my hard-fought independence would be stolen away again. I was flat out terrified.

Naturally, I did what any skittish and marginally broken creature would do when it is cornered: I panicked.

Worse, I ran.

For once I made up my mind that I was done, I was good and friggin' done. There was no talking me off the ledge, no luring me back in, no calming words to soothe me enough to stay. I followed through on my exodus and didn't think twice.

Call it selfish. Call it self-aware. Call it what you want. Just don't call it a mistake.

Looking back, I clearly see my connection with Mr. New Orleans was a symptom of my problematic engagement and a symptom of my unhappiness. I think we both confused our connection with him being a potential solution. I was so elated at being true to myself again that I allowed that same self to get pulled too deeply into something new far before I was ready. I wasn't yet me again, and I wasn't yet the partner I would need to be for a real relationship to be successful. I wasn't on the rebound per se, but I wasn't open to a new forever already, either.

I felt like I was being tested. Like the universe was asking me exactly how much I was willing to prioritize myself.

"Exactly how much have you learned?" it asked. "Exactly how much have you grown?"

In the months prior, I had repeatedly told the universe, "I choose me," so now it was asking me to prove it by walking away once again, even though it would mean breaking yet another heart.

In the end, I believe my fateful meeting with Mr. New Orleans was the universe giving me every single possible tool I needed to make the right choice for me and my future. And to his credit, Mr. New Orleans did remind me I had the strength to face my doubts head on and choose myself.

He was the exact man I needed for that season, and yet, it was not meant to be more. Unfortunately for us both, I jumped in too quickly without processing my past heartache first, thus creating a whole new heartbreak in the process. I confused the joy of living for me again with a desire to be with him. I hurt him unnecessarily, and yet didn't have the courage or the grace to say "I'm sorry" at the time. I never even gave him much closure. To put it bluntly, I fell short in every meaningful way. He gave me so much, and though I am eternally grateful, I was not then, nor will I ever be able to return the favor with the requited love he sought.

All I can do is hope that he, too, has ultimately found peace, and even more so, the love he deserves. For I am grateful every day the universe chose to put him in my path, and I am deeply thankful for the lessons learned.

Chapter 17

The Hollywood Romance

"To love oneself is the beginning of a lifelong romance."
— Oscar Wilde, *An Ideal Husband*

Wedding Countdown: Two months after

I've always been a romantic. A lover of rom-coms, Brontë novels, Jane Austen affairs, and yes, even the cheesiest films from the Hallmark movie canon. Love stories like these, realistic or imagined, absolutely make my heart swoon. I don't care how predictable or repetitive or downright absurd the plot may be. I love it when a boy, say an undercover European prince who fled to a small-town American university to escape his tacky tabloid past back home in Denmark, meets a girl, perhaps a dairy farmer's daughter who is hell-bent on getting into medical school and swears off all men for the rest of the school year, enter a seemingly unlikely scenario where they are paired as reluctant lab partners, proceed to fall in love, get discovered by the press, move back to Denmark for coronation balls galore, and live happily ever after as Mr. and Mrs. Prince Charming. OK, so this is actually the plot from the 2004 chick flick, *The Prince and Me*, but I have always trusted in the possibility of a fairytale love like that, and I find joy and comfort in fifty shades of Hollywood love eternal.

Perhaps it was because of this minor, all right major, obsession with cinematic love stories that I managed to manifest my very own Hollywood hunk. Enter Mr. Super Star.

Let me introduce the characters.

Me, a perpetually busy woman thrusting all of her time, energy, and effort into her philanthropic efforts as the co-chair of the prestigious Junior League of Denver's Annual Gala, "The Journey."

Him, a handsome, older actor of the former-model persuasion who was going to be in Denver on a book tour and had agreed to a coffee with the Junior League to discuss his potential as a good fit for the gala speaker of the year.

I think you can guess where this is going...

When I heard we were meeting Mr. Super Star for coffee and an interview I almost choked on my daily tall, blonde, no-foam almond milk latte.

"We're meeting who?!" I exclaimed excitedly to my gal pal slash Journey co-chair slash philanthropic ride or die slash hilarious friend who talks like a trucker but genuinely has a heart of gold.

"No. Freaking. Way. I loved him in...*Insert Successful Rom-Com of the 2010s here!*" I continued to fawn to The Co-Chair as she laughed at me, repeatedly.

Naturally, I had to rewatch the flick in question at home that night with The Blonde One as an attempt to reduce any potential star-struckness before our meeting a few days later. I know it sounds weird, but I swear to you, it helped! After all, he was just a man. A hunky man, but just a man, nonetheless. Admittedly, I have a penchant for truly beautiful men (remember Mr. Ex?), so it would have fit with my usual pattern to be into this man. But I was in no way interested in getting involved with anyone at the moment, let alone someone in the public sphere. Too many recently deceased skeletons in this closet, thank you very much.

Nevertheless, I am a teensy bit vain. I may not have been overtly interested in this man, but I was still going to make damn sure I looked my best for the meeting! Look good, feel good, play good, and all.

I wore a white, tennis-style, knit dress with a bright-blue, striped collar for a pop of color. It had the added benefit of making my eyes pop pretty darn good, too, if I do say so myself.

The only problem was I couldn't wear said dress on my flight to Chicago later that afternoon (no bare legs on a plane; it's my unbreakable rule and should be yours, too). I was heading straight from the meeting to visit The Single Lady for another girls' weekend, so I resigned myself to a rather undignified outfit change in the airport parking lot, but that was a later problem.

After all, I wanted to look professional, philanthropic, and somewhat serious, but definitely not boring. Appropriately housewifey, despite not being married. Casual, but chic. I was going for the cool girl, slightly uninterested look. The "I don't care if you're hot and famous, you're not getting any of this" vibe, if you will.

Then came our fateful meeting day...

INT. URBAN COFFEE SHOP–EARLY AFTERNOON

WE OPEN on a modern, local coffee shop in Denver. Huge windows illuminate the cozy space as the smell of perfectly roasted coffee wafts through the air. We see the baristas hard at work as a gaggle of gals conspiratorially lean in to chat.

Our VP of Fundraising, our Sustainer Advisor, and I all met at the local coffee shop early to strategize. We agreed we needed to hear Mr. Super Star's story, subsequently gauge the potential interest level of our audience, experience his charisma firsthand, and generally get a feel for if he was the right guy for the job or not. Easy peasy lemon squeezy.

ENTER Mr. Super Star and his book tour assistant. The Hollywood hunk strolls in the front door wearing jeans and a simple, white, V-neck T-shirt.

I'm not exaggerating here when I say he was absolutely dripping with charm and sex appeal.

Despite feeling my heart beating in my throat, I remained resolute. *You're not getting any of this, we are not interested in a new relationship, closet skeletons, remember?* Bright eyes, smile on, it was showtime all around.

Though I don't quite remember the specifics, we did in fact exchange relatively unremarkable introductions as we all shook hands and turned to order our coffees. A brief moment to catch our breaths and smooth our feathers, so to speak. It was a welcomed break from the nervous energy that was understandably swirling around all those of the female persuasion.

Once ordered, the rest of the group settled in at a few small tables we managed to haphazardly push together, and I took it upon myself to wait by the counter and deliver coffees as they came up. I tend to be overly helpful when I'm nervous.

Regular, black drip coffee, no room for cream for The Sustainer Advisor. Check.

Medium iced vanilla latte for The VP of Fundraising. Yup, got it.

The orders were rolling out and I was content to serve. I love hosting, so this was a natural role for me. Plus, it gave me something to do with my hands. It was comfortable. It was me at my best.

Two down, three to go.

Back turned to the group, I rocked my weight back and forth between my feet. Left, two, three. Right, two, three. Left, two, three, the same way I do when I wait for my luggage at baggage claim. It's not exactly a nervous tic, but it is a bit of a self-soothing sway, if you will. I was waiting patiently, slowly rocking back and forth when a voice close behind me broke my trance: "So, how's your day going?"

Startled, I turned and was even more shocked to discover the kind and genuine voice belonged to none other than Mr. Super Star himself. True to his gentlemanly ways, he said he noticed I was waiting for our coffees alone and had decided to keep me company. The gesture was considerate and generous and thoughtful and disconcerting all at once.

It was a lot, and despite myself, I blushed.

"Ohhh, uhhhh, hi. My day's good. Busy, but good. Thank you," I stammered at first, but ultimately regained my composure and even managed a natural and genuine smile.

"Glad to hear it. What do you have going on after all this?" he asked, expertly making small talk.

"I have to drive to the airport as soon as we finish." Just the facts.

"And are you going anywhere exciting?" he continued, trying to make it past my firmly fortified walls of defense.

"I'm heading to Chicago for a girls' weekend." I replied, still nothing but matter of fact.

Alas, his face lit up with a megawatt smile as he half-laughed and said, "I live in Chicago."

Large, iced, green tea for The Book Tour Assistant.

"Really?!" I gushed, "I love Chicago! It has everything a girl could want. Good food. Good shopping. All the sports teams, especially the Cubs. I mean come on, Wrigleyville? I love baseball, so I'm a big fan of Wrigleyville."

It was a bit on the chatty tour guide side, but it was true. I do love baseball, so when I naturally defaulted to talking about things I know, I sort of prattled on a bit. Mr. Super Star smiled like I had somehow amused him and politely agreed about Wrigleyville. Points for him!

Large, iced coffee for Mr. Super Star.

Unphased by the coffee orders now piling up on the counter between us, Mr. Super Star looked me straight in the eyes and continued, "You know I'd be happy to give you recommendations for Chicago, if you'd like?"

Medium, no foam, almond milk latte for Katherine.

"Umm, sure, that would be very helpful," I replied, shifting quickly, trying to pick up all three coffees that were rapidly melting into watered-down disasters.

"Let me help you," he added, as he took a cup from the balancing act in my hands and gestured for me to lead the way back to the table of women who were now intently watching this interaction. I sat demurely in my middle seat, serendipitously straight across from Mr. Super Star, as both of my friends and fellow JLDers smirked devilishly in my direction. No doubt blushing again, I passed out the coffees and offered curtly, "Shall we get started? I have a flight to catch."

Composure temporarily intact, we launched into an effortless chat about the gala. Mr. Super Star told us his personal story, offered anecdotes from his new book, gave insight into the creative process, and happily answered all of our questions. We explained the organization, our mission, our members, the goal of the fundraiser, and what we were looking for in a speaker. It was a perfectly normal, productive, and professional coffee meeting. Yay, team!

Yet, as we were wrapping up, there was once again a sudden shift in the conversation. For some unexplained reason, and completely out of nowhere, Mr. Super Star turned those dreamy eyes back to me.

"So, Chicago, get your phone out and take notes. I'm telling you where to go," he said bluntly.

Happy to have recommendations, especially about where to get good food, and disarmed by his directness, I pulled out my phone, opened a new note, and said, "OK, hit me."

By this time, I really was relaxed. I'd enjoyed hearing the story of his personal journey and appreciated his candor. It felt natural to match his fast-paced, high-frequency, creative-type energy. He was fun, for crying out loud! I welcomed what he had to offer and listened intently as he rattled off Chicago's best.

Girl and the Goat. Small plates. Hot spot.

Monteverde. Pure Italian divinity. (It was also conveniently located mere blocks from his apartment, though I didn't know this at the time.)

Momotaro. A sushi lover's paradise.

Maude's Liquor Bar. My favorite. It's this sexy little Parisian Place with dark corner booths for doing dark corner booth deeds. (OK, I may have borrowed the gist of this line from *Love Actually*, but in my mind, it's exactly what he said!)

Was it me and wishful thinking, or did each place seem to have an inkling of sex attached to it? I was particularly interested in his description of Maude's Liquor Bar. A quaint Parisian place with as yet unfulfilled sexual tension lingering in the air? With you?

Oui, monsieur.

After frantically typing in the details of his soliloquy, I set my phone back upon the table with an audible *phew*, a smile, and a satisfied thank you.

I thought our little show was over. I was wrong.

He confidently picked up my still unlocked phone and began to type. Flabbergasted, my jaw must have hit the table as I cried out in mock horror, "Excuse you! What are you doing with my phone?"

"Texting." He shrugged. Shrugged! Like it was the most obvious thing in the world.

He proceeded to text *himself* from my phone, then handed it back to me across the table. Our hands touched for just a moment, but it was long enough for electricity to run between them like a lightning rod. I almost jumped back from the jolt.

"Now I have your number, in case I think of anything else..."

That's it? That's the only explanation I get? Did Mr. Super Star really just get my number in front of all these other women? Shut the front door.

With that, he stood, and we all instinctively followed suit. Me, too stunned to do anything but play follow the leader. The others, catching his cue that this meeting was over. We gathered our things and walked to the door, which he elegantly held open, beckoning us to pass through with a graceful wave of his arm, "After you, ladies." It seems Mr. Super Star has also watched his fair share of romantic comedies.

Once outside, cordial goodbyes were exchanged by all. Then it was my turn. After hanging back in silence, I stepped forward, extending my hand professionally, my cool, calm, still trying to be uninterested vibe firmly back in place.

He shook my hand, smiling knowingly all the while, and said simply, "Talk to you soon."

Light and breezy. I made it! We're all g...

Wink.

I froze in an instant.

UGHHHHHHHHHH. Are you kidding me?! A sodding wink?! And a good wink at that. Not your average, every day, amateur wink. Nope, this was a practiced, camera-ready, spot on, hit the mark every single time, proper pretty wink, y'all.

Damn.

I was hooked. I knew he was an actor, likely playing a part even then, but I didn't care. I was picking up what he was putting down and buyin' what he was sellin'. Flattery and attention had gotten him everywhere with me, and I was officially intrigued.

Double damn.

Mr. Super Star and his assistant walked off into the sunset. OK, not really, they just walked down Holly Street, but our group of Junior League three lingered in the parking lot to debrief.

I was prepared to jump into the upcoming gala business, but as soon as Mr. Super Star was safely out of earshot, The VP of Fundraising and The Sustainer Advisor looked me dead in the eye and said simply, "WHAT. The. Hell. Was. That?"

Feigning ignorance, I replied, "What was WHAT?" More blushing.

"You know exactly what WHAT we're talking about. He was flirting with you!"

"You think?"

They raised their eyebrows at each other and simultaneously declared, "Oh, yeah!"

"I'm sure he was just acting," I protested, knowing full well he was, but also secretly hoping it wasn't entirely true.

"Probably," The Sustainer Advisor admitted. "But he also just got your number in front of three other women, so that has got to count for something."

"You think?" was apparently the only reply I could offer under such duress.

"YES!" they both sighed with exasperation once again.

"You are so texting him," The VP of Fundraising pronounced, but I was already prepared to counter.

"No, no, no. He needs to text me first," I said. "I'm sure he has hundreds of women texting him on a daily basis."

Ever the rationalist, and God bless her for it, The Sustainer Advisor simply stated, "True, but he specifically said he was looking forward to hearing from YOU. Given what you've been through the last few months, I think you deserve this. What on earth have you got to lose?"

Was she right? Did I deserve a fun and flirty fling to help this Stella get her groove back? Could this help me wade through the still mucky post-wedding-disaster dating waters? Could this experience help me learn even more about myself? Could I choose to do exactly what I wanted regardless of how others might view it?

Why the heck not? What harm could a simple *"Lovely to meet you"* text really do? This was the real world, not a movie, right? Things like this just don't happen in the real world, at least not to small town philanthropists hell-bent on hosting a successful gala and swearing off all men for the rest of the year!

I drove to the airport, fidgety, but happy. I changed into more appropriate travel clothes, and waited the few required hours–I didn't want to appear too eager–until I was settled in my seat. Then I sent the text.

"Such a pleasure to meet you today. Thank you for all of the expert recommendations. I can't wait to try them all! Have a good rest of your book tour."

Mostly neutral. Just a thank you. No questions requiring follow up but still an opening for him to reply if he so chose. I timed it perfectly, so as soon as I hit send, I turned my phone on airplane mode and got ready for takeoff. I had no interest in agonizing over whether he would respond or not, which is why I waited until just before takeoff, but in the end, I couldn't help it.

The entire flight, I waffled between hope ("maybe he will") and logic ("he probably won't"). Flip-flopping back and forth, I wasn't even totally sure I wanted him to respond. I mean, what would it even mean? A few texts? Perhaps. Continued conversations? Unlikely. A date? Not a chance in hell.

Plus, remember those skeletons of weddings past and my recently failed attempt at a relationship with Mr. New Orleans? Yeah, I didn't really want to publicly unpack those anytime soon, either. This was so not what I had in mind when I considered dipping my toe back in the dating pond, and I was already exhausted from hours of mental gymnastics before we'd even had a one-on-one conversation.

Just as I was really gaining momentum on a proper doom spiral, we landed back on solid ground with a thud. I prepared to reconnect with the real world, took a deep breath, and toggled my phone back to life.

Here we go again, I reflected, but before I could even finish the thought, I heard those glorious three notes.

Ding. Ding. Ding.

To my complete and total surprise, Mr. Super Star had not only responded, but he'd continued the exchange with a little light banter of his own. *Hmmm.* I was still timid and unsure, but he had officially piqued my interest.

Could he really be attracted to me? I wondered, as my life-long insecurities crept back to the forefront. Determined not to overanalyze, jump ahead, or get wrapped up in the storylines of his movies, I decided then and there to just enjoy the friendship for whatever it was going to be.

Thankfully, I had a feeling that, *Oh, yeah, this was going to be fun! Wink.*

* * *

The weeks went by as we slowly built a rapport. We Instagram messaged here and there, and I'd get a secret rush of adrenaline whenever I would see his blue check mark pop up on my list of likers. He'd send me flirty DMs. I'd reply in kind. Then, we upped the ante and started actually messaging IRL more and more. This was no longer just the minor league social media flirtation, y'all: we were in the big leagues of actual iMessages. Trust me, it matters.

There was no dramatic influx of "good mornings" or talking every day, rather it was a slow build in frequency and consistency of friendly communication. A slow build of "will we chat today?" or "won't we?" A slow burn.

But as fate or Hallmark would have it, I was already set to attend a bachelorette in Chicago a few weeks later for a dear friend of mine, so it was the perfect opportunity to go on an actual date and see if our meet-cute chemistry was worthy of prime time. A screen test, so to speak.

In line with our first conversation, which he somehow miraculously remembered, Mr. Super Star took the initiative to get us tickets to a Chicago White Sox game the day after the bachelorette trip ended. In a somewhat uncharacteristic leap of faith, I agreed to stay in Chicago for an extra day so we could actually go on said date. I mean, he'd already bought the tickets and all. Plus, part of me was just pumped to go to another Major League Baseball stadium, since one of my life goals is to go to a game at every single MLB stadium. I was also excited for what was sure to be a light-hearted, all-American, wholesome first date, and I really needed one of those after the intensity of the Mr. New Orleans situation.

Nevertheless, I had to survive the bachelorette first!

The gorgeous bride-to-be, the girls, and I had the absolute BEST weekend. Boat cruises on the river with megaphones, champagne, and itsy-bitsy teeny-weeny bikinis, recovery espresso shots the next morning with a lemon twist (I swear it's a thing), brunches at Hampton Social (Streeterville), rooftop views at London House, touristing at The Bean (bachelorettes love a photo op!), general shenanigans, and last but not least, an all-out '80s night at Topgolf!

Mr. Super Star and I texted continuously through it all, so eventually I was forced to come clean to the girls and tell them what was going on. Despite my attempts to hide it, they had witnessed me smiling endlessly at my phone all weekend long and knew something was up! Or rather someone was up in my inbox.

Where I thought the bachelorette gals would be taken aback, given they were friends I made through Mr. Ex, they were actually ecstatic for me. They didn't begrudge me my happiness; they were supporting it. Rooting for it, even. They, too, said it was a "must-see-him" sort of situation, so after Topgolf on our last night of the celebration, we agreed to invite him and his friends out to meet us.

To my surprise, he said they'd be there immediately.

Only then did I remember I was dressed in a hot pink floral tuxedo dress from Zara, complete with massive shoulder pads, '80s make-up, and a huge fuchsia bow in my overly hair sprayed hair.

I regretted my decision for a split-second before I thought to myself, *Welp, this is me. I love a costume, I love a theme, and I love the over-the-top fun of not giving a flip what everyone else around me thinks.* This suave, smooth, famous man would get to see the real, goofy, silly, '80s me, and I was surprisingly OK with it. I had just spent a month trying to fit into the mold of the perfect new girlfriend for Mr. New Orleans, and a full two years before trying to be the perfect fiancée and housewife-to-be for Mr. Ex. I was fresh out of give-a-shits, and I was determined not to repeat the same mistakes. I was going to be my full authentic self, and if Mr. Super Star couldn't handle me, well, then, that was just the way the cookie crumbles.

Mr. Super Star arrived while we were ordering at the bar, and I happened to look back over my shoulder at the exact moment he was making his grand entrance. I swear to you, the crowd parted, as if it was a perfectly rehearsed scene in a movie, and he smiled *that* smile as he walked purposefully my way. We hugged with a lilted "hello, again" and settled back into the bar as he took it upon himself to order us all drinks. Have I mentioned I also love a man with confidence?

Almost instantly, he was swarmed by admirers like flies on crap. Or perhaps, bees on honey is a better metaphor, given his innate sweetness. *Bogey on your six! Two more coming in hot!* I thought as I gave a mental play-by-play in my head. A middle-aged hanger-on pretended to bump his shoulder and feigned surprised when she then instantly recognized him, mock-shock spreading across her face. She tried to strike up a conversation, but Mr. Super Star politely excused himself and circled back to me.

Incoming! Fan-girl number two was even more aggressive as she batted her eyelashes and hit him with every womanly wile she had in her undeniably extensive arsenal. Still, no luck lady. Sorry.

I'm not sure how Mr. Super Star felt about it all–he was probably used to it–but I wasn't bothered in the slightest. On the contrary, I found it equal parts fascinating and flattering! Fascinating in an anthropological study of human mating rituals kind of way. Flattering because amidst *alllll* this female attention he remained solely focused on me. He genuinely wanted to hear more of my story and learn more about the real me. He saw me for me, and through this truth, I quickly realized we might actually have a connection worth exploring. So much so that I told him about writing this book, and he was nothing but supportive, though I'm not sure he ever thought he would be included within its pages.

The entire night continued to build my confidence to a level it had not seen in years, and Mr. Super Star's affections were a huge part of said boost. He liked when I laughed too loud, where others had chastised that same characteristic. He appreciated when I was a goof, where others couldn't stand it, asking me to "please be serious" during what should have been easy breezy moments. He even found the '80s costume sexy (supposedly). We somehow created our own little world within the chaos, like a peaceful bubble. He even convinced me to practice our "model walks" in the middle of the crowded, Saturday night bar. Him first, me following suit. I'm not positive why I remember this scenario in particular, but I think it's because I would NEVER dream of doing something so brazen and public in "real life." (Just ask my publisher how well this exact request went during our book cover shoot. Yikes.)

It was also a testament to my trust in him and my willingness to let loose, be silly, and be unapologetically me. It was evidence of the freedom and fun he created in those around him, and that was the sexiest thing on earth.

In no rush to end the night but nevertheless forced to say goodbye at closing time, we finalized our plans for the next day and went our separate ways.

Though I didn't think I would be able to doze off with all the flirtatious energy still racing through my body, I fell deeply asleep. Completely and totally at peace, unburdened and happy with the possibilities of tomorrow.

I woke up the next morning refreshed, but I also had proper butterflies doing 360s in the pit of my stomach. OK, maybe it was partially due to a mighty mini hangover, but it was a special feeling nonetheless. I helped get the battle-scared bachelorette ladies sober enough to board their respective planes and then showered for my own date with destiny. I put on my "casual, first-date with a movie star, but also at a baseball game, but also color-coordinated for the White Sox, but it's also kind of cold and rainy out" outfit and was ready to roll.

I Ubered to his house so we could head to the game together. My nerves were running wild like the players around the bases when a ball lands deep in center field and the tying run is on second base, and I pushed the doorbell. He buzzed me up with a cheerful, "Morning, beautiful" over the intercom, and I made my way to the front door.

I don't know what I had been expecting, but when he opened the door, I found him...brushing his teeth. It was ADORABLE. I was instantaneously disarmed and chuckled easily as he leaned toward me, toothpaste lips and all, to give me a quick kiss hello, our first kiss. It was precious and perfect and gentle and sweet. It was the break in the ice we needed, and I relaxed easily into the start of the date in a way that surprised even me.

As it turns out, I had dressed perfectly for the occasion. I wore black jeans, a black and white striped silk blouse, and a black leather jacket. Hard meets soft, classy meets edgy sort of vibe. He matched in black jeans, a plain black shirt, and a black jacket as well. Not too matchy-matchy, but still coordinated enough in a cute "we've been a couple for years and we just naturally dressed like this" sort of way.

Nailed it.

The game played out almost exactly as you would expect. Insert baseball-themed rom-com montage song here. Maybe Keith Urban's "Somebody Like You" à la *How To Lose A Guy in Ten Days*, or The Chiffons' "One Fine Day" or something like "Are You Gonna Be My Girl" by Jet to better fit our all-black ensembles and the slightly crispy fall air.

We held hands walking through the stadium, ate world-famous Chicago hot dogs, drank beers, and cheered loudly as his favorite players took the field. We laughed and snuck sweet kisses, and he even bought me a classic White Sox hat so I could fully "look the part."

While writing this chapter, I went back and watched our videos from the game and all I can hear is my own unfiltered delight and genuine (albeit loud) laughter. The laugh I have when I truly can't hold it in, when I am joyful and completely in the moment. I was light. I was happy. I was grateful to Mr. Super Star for what I thought would be an escape from reality but what turned out to be an eye-opener to the real-world amazingness I was already living in the present moment. He made me realize how blessed I already was, and he not only gave me permission to be free, he also refused to accept anything less than the flawlessly imperfect, authentic me.

It wasn't a fairytale, it was reality, and for the first time in a long time, that was so, so, so, much better.

We sat right behind the Sox bench, so I guess it's no surprise, but halfway through the game, the sweet kid behind us tapped Mr. Super Star frantically on the shoulder and shouted in his face, "You're on the Kiss Cam!"

So much for anonymity...

We obliged with a quick, family-friendly kiss and as the crowd cheered and I blushed, Mr. Super Star reached over and grabbed my hand, smiling gently and reassuringly my way.

I guess it was a fairytale after all.

In the coming weeks, subsequent dates followed. We indulged at the places he had recommended in our fateful coffee shop meeting back in Denver, including the sexy Parisian place, Maude's, which fully lived up to its promises of sexual tension. We attended art shows, roaming about and discussing the artistic process we both respected. We met friends, shared more romantic meals, kissed everywhere, despite being photographed at times by random fans. We took selfies, went to very sweaty yoga, shopped and meandered around town, laughing all the while. Then we stayed in, lounged on the couch, and watched *Band of Brothers* from the comfort of his home, dissecting the cinematography and production techniques before we inevitably got distracted by kissing, and often more. We were normal.

It was perfectly fun and carefree. No pressure on either side, but also no progress.

Mr. Super Star made me feel sexy, told me I was beautiful, and even (gasp) valued my goofy persona and uniquely curious brain. He helped me remember to have fun and showed me the romance I had been craving for years. Yearrrs, people.

Hell, he gave me my very own Hollywood rom-com, y'all!

We were well-matched as an "almost couple," but in the end, we weren't made to go the distance. Unlike most endings, though, ours was not fraught with conflict or fights or drama. It sounds odd to say, but we just happily drifted apart, growing in different directions, each flourishing and thriving in our own ways.

He was busy acting, and I was busy putting my life and myself back together. We both needed to remain focused on our own stuff, so that was all she wrote. No harm, no foul. Just joy and memories of laughter and the reminder being my freest and most authentic self in a relationship is not a luxury, it's a requirement. It was proof of my growth, and proof I was one step closer to the me I'd always wanted to be.

I still squeal with excitement when I see his successes on the big or little screens, and we remain good friends through it all. In the end, although our story wasn't quite motion picture perfect, it was pretty darn close.

Furthermore, it reminded me of the romance I wanted in my life: the laughter, the joy, the chemistry, the fun, the silly, the genuine. It showed me that my romance novel dreams were possible and expanded my vision of relationships, allowing me to believe I could have what my heart wished for after all. It reminded me why I had refused to settle, and it reignited my hope for the endless possibilities my future might hold.

In that sense, I guess it really was a happily ever after for us both after all.

Chapter 18

The Final Test

"The biggest adventure you can ever take
is to live the life of your dreams."
– Oprah Winfrey, *O, The Oprah Magazine*

Wedding Countdown: Three months after
Last, but not least, and certainly not to be outdone, there was one final test headed my way in the form of Mr. Tech Mega Millions, a wildly successful, and even more impressively brilliant, tech entrepreneur from Silicon Valley.

I was minding my own business one lazy Saturday evening, making dinner at home in the same kitchen I'd previously shared with Mr. Ex and the site of our final breakup, and texting lightly with one of my oldest and most revered college besties, Mr. Diva Curls. It was pretty innocuous banter per usual about what else but baseball once again (which he happens to hate as much as I love), until he asked coyly if he could introduce me to one of his longtime friends and business associates from Silicon Valley. I was dubious at best given that I was still hot off the heels of not only a failed engagement, but also a rather unsuccessful attempt to reenter the dating pool with Mr. New Orleans, and then a slow drift away from Mr. Super

Star. Understandably, I wasn't positive I was ready to try again so soon.

Mr. Diva Curls reassured me that not only was said mystery man smart, well-traveled, educated, and driven, but perhaps most pragmatic of all, he was already very interested in meeting me. Since I'd trust Mr. Diva Curls with my life, I agreed to him passing along my mobile number, but I wasn't overly optimistic this somewhat set-up would actually result in a text, let alone a date. I figured Mr. Diva Curls was out on the town and the most likely outcome was we would probably laugh about this exchange a few days later.

Imagine my surprise when all of eighty-two seconds later my phone was ringing with an unknown San Francisco area code. Not a text, a real live phone call, people. Since I knew my potential date was from Cali, I broke my normal pattern of unknown number screening and answered the call. Happily, I was greeted with the standard "BOLLLTTT CUTTERRRS" scream from my bestie himself. Mr. Diva Curls has known me for decades and has *endless* variations of nicknames for me: Bumble Bolt, Bolt Cutters, Bolty Bolt. You get the picture.

Apparently, Mr. Diva Curls and the mystery man were actually together at the bar in New York, so once the required "Bolt Cutters" chant was out of the way, the mystery man took the phone and said, "Hello."

"Hello there," I replied with slight shock and, for some reason, a lot of nervous energy as I stood there dumbstruck in my own kitchen, wooden spoon still in hand.

"Our mutual friend tells me you are pretty amazing, and I was hoping to take you out this weekend."

Confused and completely caught off guard by the directness of his approach, I managed to answer with what I considered to be a fairly important clarifying question, given it was currently Saturday night and unless I was mistaken there was only one day left in said weekend, "Aren't you currently in New York?"

"Don't worry about it," he countered. "Are you free tomorrow or not?"

"As a matter of fact, I am."

"Good. I'll text you in a bit with a plan."

"Um, OK, but what exactly are we doing?" I asked, still baffled at this rapid turn of events, and totally lacking an understanding of how the logistics of this now agreed upon date for the next day could possibly play out.

"Let me worry about that. I'll see you tomorrow."

And just like that, he hung up, and my relationship with Mr. Tech Mega Millions was born.

I stood in my kitchen, mystified but intrigued. What on earth had I just agreed to!? Who was this mysterious man, and more importantly, what would I need to wear? I mean, I appreciated his confidence and all, but I certainly did not appreciate the lack of information.

Thankfully, a few hours later he made good on his promise and texted me with his plan.

He had already chartered a private jet (yup, you read that right) to fly him direct from NYC to DEN first thing in the morning so we could attend the time-honored tradition of a Sunday afternoon Broncos game. He said he had already bought the tickets, so there was no room for argument, even if I had wanted to. How men seem to grasp that Sports with a capital S is one of the fastest ways to my heart, I will never know, but I'm not complaining. (Though now that I think of it, Mr. Diva Curls may have had a hand in that one!)

Anyhow, after the game we would have a casual dinner, reservations already secured.

I guess it's settled then, I thought.

What I texted was a short, "Can't wait."

After all, I love it when a plan comes together.

We had agreed to meet on neutral turf for a pre-game drink at The Four Seasons bar in downtown Denver. I guess it's not really neutral turf when one person is a regular at the place, but I sure as hell didn't tell him that. I was fine with a little homefield advantage.

I walked in the door and Mr. Tech Mega Millions (Mr. TMM for short) immediately stood to greet me. He knew me from a picture Mr. Diva Curls had shown him, and I appreciated the gentlemanly gesture of standing as I, a lady, entered the room. We are about the same height, so his electric blue eyes instantly locked dead on mine–*dang*–and we exchanged the continental greeting of an air kiss on each cheek. Through some light Google stalking, I knew Mr. TMM had gone to university in England and had lived abroad in Europe for many years, so I was prepared for either a one or two cheek-kissing situation.

"Shall we sit?" he asked a bit shakily.

I was glad to see he was as nervous as me.

"Our mutual friend tells me you're finishing your MBA, how's it going?" He kicked the conversation off immediately, and even though it gave off slight job interview vibes, from there we chatted nonstop for over an hour.

Educational backgrounds, work histories, travel bucket lists, recently read books, brief family overviews–we covered all the basics. I quickly realized that on paper, we were well matched, and he seemed to think the same. He smiled warmly and exuded genuine excitement as we left for the game.

I'm familiar with the Broncos' stadium, so I was ready to lead the way through what I assumed were unfamiliar waters. But my mental prep turned out to be completely unnecessary as Mr. Tech Mega Millions, despite never having been to a Broncos game, was unphased by the commotion and self-assuredly guided *me* through the crowded concourse. We picked up a few bevvies and took our seats. I was legitimately ready to watch the game, prepared to comment on strategy, bad calls, and the like, but Mr. Tech Mega Millions had other ideas. He was ready to discuss wine, like my grandfather's favorite red, food, more travel tales, and the arts. I happily acquiesced. Far be it from me to deny someone the finer things in life. Fine dining and culture it was!

For the life of me, I do not remember if the Broncos won or lost that day. I was genuinely enjoying Mr. Tech Mega Millions' worldly point of view and intelligent conversation. Furthermore, if I'm being honest, I was intimidated by it. I've been privileged enough to explore my fair share of incredible places in this world, and I like to think I'm pretty well-educated, but when I was up against an expat with a PhD from one of the top universities in the United Kingdom, I didn't feel like I had all that much to offer. He was just so dang smart!

Fortunately, he liked me anyway.

We continued our marathon first date with dinner at a local tapas restaurant. He surprised me with a bottle of my grandfather's favorite wine–ten points for a good memory–

and ordered way too many dishes for us to share. Now, I don't mind being doted upon, what woman does? But I was a bit thrown off when he ordered all our food without even asking me what I liked, wanted, could or couldn't eat. Not a total deal breaker, but it was a bit much on night one.

Given it was our first date and I could sense he was still trying to make the best possible impression, I chalked it up to a first date faux pas. After having to take care of every single little thing for the last three years, it was actually nice to not have to think about what to order.

I dismissed the minor second thoughts and settled in for another three-hour long session of brand new relationship getting to know each other chit chat. We hit the deeper subjects this time—further familial disclosures, me calling off my wedding, other failed relationships, general dating history, hopes for the future, wildest dreams—you know, typical first date fodder. We genuinely hit it all. It was a little deep and a little fast, but he was honest and forthcoming, so I was charmed rather than concerned.

On the whole, the date went well enough, and we agreed to see each other again. I had to go to him this time, though.

* * *

With Phantom Planet's "California" playing on repeat in my mind, I prepared to journey west.

We picked a weekend only a few weeks away and Mr. Tech Mega Millions set about planning yet another surprise. It was late October, so packing for an as-yet-undisclosed California locale presented a serious wardrobe problem. I was finally able to convince him to divulge we were going somewhere on the coast, thus nixing the need for the more robust puffers, sweaters, and boots, but as I boarded the plane to San Francisco, I still had no idea where we would actually end up. Again, not the worst problem in the world, since I was so genuinely thrilled someone other than me had taken the planning reins for once!

Ever the provider, he picked me up at San Francisco International Airport and even carried my bags to his car, loading the heavy suitcases in the SUV, which he said he drove because he knew I would overpack.

I mean, he wasn't wrong.

We headed south and he was finally forced to give in to my repeated whining of, "Are we there yet? Are we there yet?"

"Relax, it's only a two-hour drive to Monterey."

"Monterey?!?" I squealed with unbridled excitement as I clapped my hands with childlike joy.

"But first, I need to take a work call. Do you mind if we pull over close by? You can get out and explore while I take the call in private."

"Of course! Let's stop there!" I exclaimed as I pointed to a road sign reading Hellyer County Park. I could entertain myself in a pretty park for an hour or so, don't you worry, buddy.

We parked in the mostly empty parking lot and I hopped out to explore. There was a stunning lake, like glass, with swans swimming languidly about. It was still cool in the fall morning air, but my shawl and the sun made it bearable, so I took my book with me as I searched for the perfect spot to perch. I even heard Mr. Tech Mega Millions laugh as I sauntered exaggeratedly away.

He pulled out his phone, and it was time for business.

I stumbled upon an unbearably beautiful bench, just at the water's edge. The worn wooden planks were already heated from the California sunshine, and it was symmetrically flanked by sculptural cattails gently swaying in the breeze. I heard the wind softly whisper through the leaves of the oak tree above me and it smelled faintly of dewy grass as I took a deep, calming inhale. As I sighed out what felt like the last ounce of long-held tension in my body, I curled up like a cat in my new Garden of Eden, opened my book, and was immediately at peace. Complete and total perfection.

It was one of those moments where time both stood still and flew by swiftly. Completely engrossed in my book and focused solely on the task of enjoying myself, I hardly clocked that forty-five minutes had passed in an instant.

"Katherine!"

Startled, I let out a tiny gasp of a scream, which was quickly followed by a wholehearted chuckle as I threw my head back and laughed, bringing both of my hands to my heart as I often do when I am caught off guard.

Mr. Tech Mega Millions sat down next to me, bent forward with his elbows resting on his knees, and looked at me sideways with a warm smile.

"I took a picture of you while I was on my call," he said gently, almost bashful.

"Oh, really?" I was taken aback, but curious.

"Yeah, I was on my call, and I looked over at you and it stopped me in my tracks. You just looked so serene and beautiful."

"Wow, OK, I don't even know what to say. But thank you, I think. Can I see it?" I asked equally as timidly.

He held out the latest iPhone model and sure enough, my image filled the screen.

Arm casually draped over the back of the bench with my knees pulled up to the side in my leopard knee-length skirt. Sunglasses on, reading calmly. Just a hint of my pearl-covered, pointy-toe flats peeking out from between the wooden planks. Not a soul around. Framed by oak after stately oak with the lake as a mirrored backdrop. I looked so in my element. So calm, so at peace.

Just so very much like me.

It took me a minute to take it all in, but sure enough, he had captured all of me. Like an impressionist oil painting come to life, there I was, vulnerable, relaxed, dare I say beautiful.

He captured the essence of who I am in private, when all my guards are down and when I am most open and true. The authentic me.

Surprising even myself, soft, happy tears began to well up in the corners of my eyes. They didn't crescendo into a full fall down my ample cheeks, but as I looked back at him, he could see the subtle, tell-tale glisten in my eyes. I wasn't crying because *I* looked so beautiful, no, that's not what gets me. I was crying because the *moment* he captured was so beautiful, the feeling so special, and the peace so absolutely unbreakable. The truth he captured was utterly raw and rare.

"Thank you," I almost whispered.

It wasn't much in the way of grand speeches, but it was all I could muster in the moment. I couldn't, or perhaps wouldn't, for fear of breaking the spell, explain why the photo touched my heart so much, but I like to think he understood my deep gratitude and the bigness contained in that small, quiet moment.

There's power in peace like that.

I still have the photo in the archives of my own phone, but I don't need it. If I close my eyes, I can feel every ounce of that glorious moment in time. The cool breeze, the warming sun upon my skin, and the smell of the still damp grass. My deep, appreciative breaths, and the knowledge that life was good. I was completely happy in my own skin. It was the moment where I knew I was living as my authentic self, and I finally didn't feel guilty for enjoying it. I felt peace on the other side of the disaster I had emerged from and the courage to embrace it all, prioritize it all, experience it all, flipping live it all to the fullest.

That I will never forget.

Detour complete, we checked in at our hotel in Monterey Bay and scooted quickly over to Carmel-By-The-Sea. Aimless wanderings, local boutique shopping, and, of course, wine tastings were up first!

My favorite shop of the entire trip was a small home goods store already in the full swing of the upcoming Christmas season. It was overrun with décor and ornaments and tinsel and bric-à-brac of every possible persuasion, and it was heavenly. I perused the trinkets, commenting and touching almost every single item along the way, until I unearthed a long-forgotten antique ornament and knew she had to be mine. When you know, you know. You know?

I think Mr. Tech Mega Millions was expecting me to pick out something far more glamorous or at least more practical from the endless shopping options of Carmel. Instead, I picked a chintzy little $10 ornament, which he graciously paid for. He was perplexed and I was pleased. Go figure.

The next day, Mr. TMM booked us a whale watching experience on the bay. I previously mentioned to him in passing about my significant phase as a child where all I wanted to be when I grew up was a marine biologist, and yet again, he paid superb attention to detail.

You see, I am a lifelong nerd, and proud of it! Intellectual pursuits genuinely bring me joy and I am forever curious. I got the feeling Mr. TMM dug this about me, but I still couldn't bring myself to share the very embarrassing truth that as a kid, I used my Disney autograph book to take notes about various species of fish in the aquariums at Disney World instead of getting actual character autographs. Now, I may be older and marginally less obsessed, but I've never lost my love of the sea and all its creatures, so Mr. TMM hit the nail on the head with this one.

I insisted we stand outside in the chilled sea air for the entire cruise so we could better hear the informative tidbits the captain shared over the ship's intercom. I even dropped my own knowledge bombs on Mr. TMM, rambling on and on about various creatures of the sea. Perhaps he was genuinely impressed by my loquacious marine mammal commentary, but I'm guessing not. He did at least humor my amateur expertise by also taking me to the famous Monterey Bay Aquarium.

We saw graceful sharks and ever-moving schools of fish that appeared to breathe as a single organism. We touched starfish and sea cucumbers and observed ethereal jellyfish floating in an eternal current. We even waited an extra half hour to see the penguin information session because they are without a doubt my number one favorite animal of all time, ever. I also claim they are my spirit animal–awkward, but disarming, goofy but cute, and surprisingly athletic at times–but I admit this might be just wishful thinking.

I could get used to this, I thought to myself.

That night, we went back to Carmel for dinner at the delicious little Mediterranean restaurant, Porta Bella Carmel. With its picturesque, thatched roof, warm Venetian plaster walls, crates of wine lining the stairs, and candlelit tables for two, it was straight out of a Tuscan dream. Unsurprisingly, Mr. TMM had called ahead and reserved the finest and most romantic seat in the house.

As was becoming somewhat customary, I had barely even glimpsed at the menu when he proceeded to order the whole kit and kaboodle.

"We'll each start with a glass of Nicolas Feuillatte champagne, please, followed by a bottle of the 2019 1er Cru from Burgundy with dinner." He took a deep breath and proceeded, undeterred. "To eat, we'll share the steamed mussels *au vin blanc* with plenty of bread on the side and the grilled Spanish octopus, followed by the pan-seared sea scallops and the grilled king salmon. You know, salmon really is so good for you." The last was a short aside as he glanced my way. "For dessert, we'll finish with the *assiette de fromage*, please." (Two points for proper pronunciation.) "A nice cheese plate really should be the dessert course, not a starter, in my opinion." Again, an aside for my benefit, though I do completely and totally agree on this one.

It was like one long, practiced speech.

I'll admit, he ordered spectacularly well, but still, what if I had wanted the jumbo lobster ravioli, as was recommended by the waiter, or the *pappardelle alla bolognese*, which is in *my* humble opinion well and truly one of the most perfect dishes ever created?

What if I wanted to show off a little myself?

I mean, I know food. I know wine. I'm cultured. Too bad, so sad, not today, darlin'.

Having ordered our full meal and drink selections, he finally looked back in my direction, anticipating an overjoyed response. Unfortunately for him, I didn't love having my say in the matter disregarded, and having never tasted mussels before, I wasn't immediately enthused.

So, I told him, "You know, I've never actually eaten a mussel, soooo I'm not sure about that one."

"Don't worry, you'll love it," he responded, unphased.

"But what if I don't want them?"

"Well, you still have to try them."

"Seriously?"

"Yes, no arguing." He was going to make me eat the slimy little suckers whether I liked it or not.

Looking back, I know he genuinely enjoyed showing me something new, but he also appeared to get some strange satisfaction at being able to tell me what to do. To his credit, I was letting him. But I wasn't exactly comfortable with the emerging dynamic, either. It was like he didn't need me to be my most amazing version of self. He was fine with mediocre Katherine and didn't really expect me to step up to his level. I'm not saying he thought I was *less than*, but I don't think he expected me to be *as good as*. I'm a smarty-pants badass, too, and I wanted to be on par with all of his insanely amazing humanness. Yes, I wanted to be wined and dined, but I wanted to show my marvelousness, too. I wanted him to want the best of me so we could both grow into better people, rather than stagnate in good enough.

But back to the mussels–they really were divine. I'm ravenous now just thinking about them, for these little morsels now rank in the top five on my all-time favorite foods list. Good thing I didn't protest too much after all.

He was right. He knew it. *Harrumph.*

* * *

With Carmel-by-the-Sea and Monterey Bay now well and fully explored, we spent the next day driving down 17-Mile Drive with the windows down and the salty air whipping at my hair. We parked and walked along Pebble Beach, me twirling my way down the path, overcome with my love of the ocean, and Mr. TMM trailing behind, no doubt wondering who this overly energetic woman was.

He indulged my curiosity with good humor and even drove me to the iconic Bixby Bridge. I was obsessed with the show *Big Little Lies* and was blown away by its beauty in the full California technicolor of real life.

Alas, with more secret plans already in the works, we had to leave the cool comfort of the coast and head back to the city. Look out, San Francisco!

Before I left for California, Mr. TMM told me to bring a "fancy outfit" for a surprise night out. So of course, I packed not one but two options: a demure, black, floor-length dress with fluttery silk cap sleeves and a playful, white, long-sleeved mini dress with black-beaded fringe at the hem. One serious and elegant, one young and fun. I bet you can guess which one he chose based on our now well-established roles: young and fun it was.

Up first was a show, which was fantastic, but we were forced to leave early if we wanted to make our late-night dinner reservation at "his" restaurant. Well, it wasn't entirely "his," but I guess one of the perks of being a partial owner in a culinary endeavor is you do get to call it "your" restaurant. You also get to walk in an hour past your reservation time when they are about to close the doors for the night and still have a full-on private dining experience complete with a four-course meal and wine pairing. What was the concept of the restaurant, you ask?

Every single dish was made with Wagyu. Literally. Every. Single. Bite. Wagyu tartare. Wagyu-fried broccoli. Marinated and grilled Wagyu filet. Wagyu rice. Even the flourless chocolate cake was made with, you guessed it, Wagyu fat. It was decadence galore, and I was overwhelmed, to say the least. And I'm not just talking about my resulting gastrointestinal distress.

Now, I admit I love the finer things in life, but this was over-the-top rich, even by my standards. I was filled with gratitude for the experiences he was sharing with me, but I was also a bit dubious about the strings that seemed to be securely attached. Though he never outright said it, little things, like making sure I was dressed appropriately, ordering for me, keeping plans confidential, keeping me on my back foot, all raised tiny yet vibrant red flags. I fought to ignore them for the time being as he had already planned and purchased our next two dates, but once again, I had doubts.

We were booked on a sojourn to Boston two weeks later to see the mutual friend who had set us up in the first place (see Mr. Diva Curls above), followed closely by a trip to Europe two weeks after that. Two trips in four weeks. Optimistic? Very. A bit aggressive? Yeah, kinda. I felt like we were arbitrarily rushing through the phases of a relationship in the course of mere weeks and the momentum showed zero signs of slowing down. In truth, despite the marathon getting-to-know-you conversations every time we were together, Mr. TMM and I hardly knew each other, and yet he had planned one of the most amazingly romantic trips of a lifetime back to the very place where I had gotten engaged the year before.

Whoaaaa, Nelly. This was too much. Way, way too much. Too much and too soon.

My former fiancé, Mr. Ex, like Mr. TMM, had always been intense, and the previous five months of my life had been dominated for the most part by complete and total turmoil. So, the similarities, the control, the undivided attention, and the speed at which Mr. Tech Mega Millions wanted to race through the necessary steps of a healthy relationship was, well, suffocating.

To be abundantly clear, Mr. TMM did genuinely care for me, and I for him.

He wanted to protect me.

He wanted to support me and my dreams. He flat-out spoiled me.

He offered to hire a ghostwriter for this book so I "wouldn't have to work so hard," which I found only marginally insulting.

He even offered to move me and my dog, Gucci, into one of his houses in Atherton, California, so I could be close by and yet not have to worry about the cost of living in one of the most expensive zip codes in all of the United States. He essentially offered to finance, manage, and run every aspect of my life.

To be fair, these grand gestures were his way of showing he cared, and it would have been theoretically easy to say yes. Parts of me relished the admiration and the rush of serotonin brought on by such lavish attention, and I knowingly accepted. There was a part of me that still felt like I was getting something I needed, but wasn't able to unconditionally give myself just yet: deep and abiding and never-ending love.

There was also financial stability. Whereas Mr. Ex lacked the level of drive and ambition I craved in a partner, Mr. TMM showcased success in spades. He was a man with a plan and the means to see it through. He was a man who matched my intellectual curiosity and unquenchable thirst to experience the world, and his affection was intoxicating. Like I said, great on paper.

The problem was Mr. TMM had recently begun his own healing journey and, through no fault of his own, he was battling some pretty serious inner demons. He needed, and quite frankly deserved, a level of patience and support and dedication I just wasn't capable of giving only a few weeks in. He clearly had growth left to achieve, and I was done fixing folks. I had done my own hard work, made my own hard life choices, and I needed someone who had already done the same.

In addition, though I'm not sure it was intended as such, the whole situation felt somewhat controlling and if I'm honest, a little love-bomby. To me, his level of intensity felt like obsession, like possession, and I was unwilling to feel owned. I was unwilling to lose myself again in a partnership not meant for me.

For, once again, it wasn't about the stuff! It wasn't about the money or the things or the trips and gifts or the attention or how good we were on paper. They weren't the point. The point was me and what I wanted in a relationship.

The hard part was that I was incredibly thankful to Mr. TMM. He allowed me to see so many positive aspects of a relationship. He showed me I could be loved and adored and cherished and pursued. I could find an intellectual equal with equal zest for life. I could find someone to wander the world with. I could have everything I wanted and deserved with him, so long as I was willing to settle on the rest.

Was I willing to take all the good enough he had to offer and overlook the obvious issues? Was I willing to settle for an almost perfect fit, that was almost too good to be true? Or was I willing to fight for it, willing to wait, and willing to trust my gut in the process?

Could I pass this final test, showing myself and the universe alike that I was finally ready for the future I so desired?

Could I really choose myself again?

I had just fought tooth and nail to regain control of my own life, my own destiny, and I feared continuing on the pre-planned path with Mr. TMM would bring me right back to where this book started, literally. Or worse, engaged to the wrong person yet again. So, when push came to shove, or rather when push to move in after only one month of dating came to shove, I was out.

With a heavy heart, knowing the hurt I was about to inflict, I broke it off with Mr. Tech Mega Millions mere days before the Boston vacay and a few weeks before our trip abroad.

Unsurprisingly, he took it poorly. I won't go into the details, but let's just say it clarified I had indeed made the right choice once again.

* * *

In the end, none of the three incredible men I dated after Mr. Ex were my forever person. Yet, despite the flaws in our respective pairings...

Mr. New Orleans saw who I truly was and helped me face the doubts I ran from for months. He helped me realize I needed to live for me, trusting myself and my intuition above all else.

Mr. Super Star revived the romance in my life and gave me the confidence to live free, without regret, taking chances on what I authentically desired. He helped me love myself, unconditionally and without apology.

Mr. Tech Mega Millions showed me I was worth the effort. He reignited my spirit of adventure and reaffirmed my commitment to myself, my own needs, and my right to make my own choices, no matter the outcome. He helped me pass my final test.

I don't regret a single moment with any of them, though given my often clumsy and hurtful handling of our partings, I'm not entirely confident they have the same positive feelings.

In the end, I truly can't see my story being written any other way than with these three men, these three relationships, these three "failures." And still, despite this unending gratitude, there was no way in hell I was settling for anything less than my soulmate, my lover, and my best friend all rolled into one.

I *FINALLY* knew what I wanted.

And most importantly, I was *FINALLY* ready to receive it.

Chapter 19

"I Believe in a Thing Called Love"

"Remember tonight, for it is the beginning of always."
– Dante Alighieri

Given the outcome of my royally failed engagement, you may think I regret my relationship with Mr. Ex, or regret saying yes to his proposal, or, at the very least, regret not calling off the wedding sooner than two weeks prior. If you do fall into the "I assume she regrets it all" camp, then I'm sorry to disappoint you, but you're flat-out wrong. I do not regret any of it. I refuse to regret a single moment of my past.

Let me repeat myself: I. Do. Not. Regret. A. Single. Thing.

I may still be saddened by certain things, and I am most certainly sorry for certain uncharacteristic actions and the hurt I caused others, but regret? On the contrary, words simply cannot describe how truly grateful I am for all I went through, all I overcame, and all of my hard-fought growth, subsequent reflections, and life lessons learned. Need I go on? Still, I will try to put pen to paper and explain a bit more what I mean when I proclaim my deep gratitude.

Throughout the struggles, the hardships, the heartbreak, the difficult conversations with friends and family, the hurtful interactions with Mr. Ex, the unexpected meltdowns, breakdowns, and sob fests, the embarrassment, the shame, the guilt for hurting the man I once loved, the guilt for wasting money, the guilt for moving on, the guilt, the guilt, the guilt...throughout it all, there was so much more.

There was also growth, support, personal discovery, freedom from societal pressures I didn't even realize I had internalized, authenticity, a deeper relationship with myself, newfound confidence, joy, hope, and yes, even love. So, so, so much overwhelming, life-affirming, unconditional love for myself and those I cherish.

Brianna Wiest sums it up perfectly in her own book about personal transformation, *The Pivot Year*:

> *If you could make a list of everything you've ever worried about—everything you thought you'd never get over, every answer you thought you'd never find, every fear you thought would be the end of you—you'd realize that every single one passed. Despite your doubt, and despite your disbelief, a way forward was made. As time goes on, you will begin to see the magic in the process. You will begin to understand why things had to unfold precisely the way they did. You will realize that if you did not have the exact experiences you had just as you had them, you would have missed out on the essential lessons, tools, and pieces of wisdom that built you into the person you are today—the person who will keep walking you forward.` When you look back on the past, you can see purpose in how everything came to be, regardless of the twists and turns that brought you there.*

To me, it's going through the hard things, the struggles and the strife, that ultimately help you realize who you are and force you to examine your history, patterning, shortcomings, and faults. Going through things like calling off a wedding are truly the essence of the process of becoming. For really, that's all life is: the process of becoming the most authentic version of you.

Despite the turmoil of the journey, in the end, I learned more about my own code for life, my truths, and the desires of my heart in my own personal pivot year than I did in any relationship or period prior. I learned who I am and what I want for my future. I learned how to speak up for myself, prioritizing my non-negotiables even when it was excruciatingly difficult. I found my voice, and with it, I fought for what I deserve in my life and my partner. I realized what I am worthy of, and I learned how to be a better version of Katherine on the whole. In short, I became me.

I burnt it all so I could rebuild a better, stronger, and truer future. I scorched the whole dang earth of my life, and I felt every ounce of the devastating pain, hurt, and despair I caused. Hell, I even shared in the same depression I may have caused my exes over the years, but I still cannot regret what happened.

I do apologize for hurting people. Over and over and sincerely and profoundly, I apologize for the hurt, but I will never apologize for the choices I knew I had to make. Apologizing for those would be admitting I did the wrong thing, made a wrong choice, or didn't follow the right path for me personally, and I wholeheartedly believe I did what was needed to get me to where I am today.

I admit I likely handled it all so very, very poorly, but I hope one day you understand I had to roast those "good enough" relationships to a charred crisp of smoldering embers. I had to scorch those earths. I had to burn it all down to make way for my more loving, true, and beautiful future. I owed it to myself to create space for a bigger love, and in the process, I'm guessing I also made space in my exes' lives for their Mrs. Meant To Bes as well.

Because, to be abundantly clear, I am still a staunch believer in marriage, not as a societal construct and institution, necessarily, but as a *person,* where one day I can feel happy, safe, and secure. A place where I can not only be my authentic self and my own primary relationship, but also be embraced for both the wonderful and dreadfully bad pieces of my soul in equal measure.

A place where I can marry the man of my dreams because I am the woman of his. My best friend, my adventure buddy, my ride or die, my lover, my protector, my rock, my other half, my partner.

My Love.

I believe in that hope, and by choosing myself over all others, I believe I made such a future possible.

* * *

At the outset of the book, I told you we were starting at the end–the disaster of my failed wedding. And we did...sort of. For as it turns out, calling it off was only my beginning...

Remember The Matchmaker's words of wisdom from my embarrassing sob fest on the plane to my Hawaiian un-honeymoon? Well, it's time you know how she got her name...

The Matchmaker and I had been friends for many years. We met at an Emerging Leaders Habitat for Humanity Build, and she, The Wild One, and I clicked immediately. Perhaps it was the matching pink tool belts, or the instantaneous recognition of a kindred spirit, or the undeniable truth that she was my soulmate in girlfriend form who was destined to be a part of my life forever. Either way, from the very first sip of our celebratory post-construction cocktails, we were sisters. Her daughter even looks like me and refers to me as her best friend, which I am certain means something in the cosmic meant-to-be-family sort of way!

Anyhow, it was late one August day in 2019 when, in an attempt to beat the stifling Colorado summer heat, The Matchmaker and I took her kiddo on an excursion to the Denver Museum of Nature & Science. I used to work at DMNS and was ecstatic to show her daughter, my doppelganger, The Little One, all the absolutely magical hidden gems of the museum I called home. We started in the Coors Gems & Minerals Hall (vastly underrated, in my opinion), and it took all of five minutes of wandering past glistening specimens before The Matchmaker revealed her ulterior motive for this little day date.

Pushing the buggy while I lifted The Little One to get a closer look, The Matchmaker "casually" asked if I was dating again.

Now, The Matchmaker isn't exactly known for her subtlety, so when I say "casually," what I mean is she turned straight toward me and pretty much demanded an answer to her query. I looked her way as she purposefully turned back to the display in an effort to avoid my gaze.

"Yup, I'm back in the game. Why do you ask?" I inquired suspiciously.

"Oh, no reason, I just know a guy I think you would really like." She tried to slow play her excitement, but then she really couldn't help herself and continued on without waiting for a response. "He's amazing actually. He's a regular at Urban Farmer and he's kind and smart and successful and tall and loves to travel and he's an incredible skier and I just think you two would be perfect for each other. I showed him your Instagram and he thinks you're beautiful, but I wanted to check with you first before giving him your number." She exhaled forcefully in an attempt to catch her breath after this long-winded spiel. (I'd later come to find out this man also defended The Matchmaker one night when two guys made her cry at the bar where she worked, so he was a literal knight in shining armor, too.)

I laughed easily, a bit taken aback by such an effusive pitch but also intrigued by her description of this so-called amazing, kind, world-traveling skier man.

"Show me his Instagram then, too, that seems only fair," I countered.

We stood in the exhibit giggling at the phone like schoolgirls for longer than I'd like to admit. His grid lacked curation, but what it lacked in aesthetic consistency it made up for in content: skiing, mountain biking, vintage car rides, nature, art, more skiing, traveling to remote and captivating locales, skiing again, and generally adventures galore. His passions were on display for all to see, and they were as varied and exciting as my own. There was also one particularly titillating photo of him rock climbing, which perfectly highlighted a chiseled back, ample quads, and adrenaline junkie tendencies to boot. Bonus! Never mind there was nary a photo where I could actually see his face beyond what was visible around his ski goggles.

Still, sensing a potential kindred spirit, I said, "Why the hell not? Go ahead and give him my number."

She squealed, literally, clearly delighted her efforts may bear fruit.

"But I'm NOT reaching out to him," I continued. "If he wants to have a shot with me, then he has to make the first move."

"Fair," she reassured me as she bounced in place with excitement.

We continued on with the rest of our museum explorations, me determined not to bring up my potential date again for fear of getting overly hopeful, and her, dying to talk more about this mystery man while we dug for dinosaur bones in the Discovery Zone. We settled somewhere in the middle with a few more offhand comments about said human, but as I drove away at the end of the day, I decided to put Mr. Potentially Perfect out of my mind. For a) there was no guarantee he would ever call and b) there was even less of a guarantee we would actually hit it off. Plus, I was dating some other pretty great humans at the time, so even if he never called, I figured it was no great loss on my end.

* * *

Wedding Countdown: Five months after

Months went by. Yes, you read that right, *months*! No text, no DM, no call, no nothing. I'd go visit The Matchmaker at Urban Farmer for my weekly treat-yourself-to-a-glass-of-wine moment, and each time she would ask, "Anything yet?"

"Still nothing," I'd reply, which legitimately began to piss her off, I think.

She'd tell me that Mr. Potentially Perfect stopped by the day before and somehow, we had just missed each other once again. *Shrug.* Timing can be a real pain, huh? She told me she was pushing him to reach out, but he had no interest in sliding into my DMs like a super creep. I respected his restraint, and I believed that if it was meant to be, then the universe would figure out a way to work it out when the timing was right. I had bigger fish to fry, like completing the necessary finals for my graduation from the University of Denver with my professional MBA in marketing. Woo hoo!

It was November 15, 2019, exactly five months after I was supposed to get married, and I could feel it was a big, big, big moment for my future. I first started my MBA program before Mr. Ex and I were even engaged, so finally completing the program was about far more than a degree to me. It was the finale to my last remaining chapter involving Mr. Ex, and I felt like I was graduating in every possible sense of the word.

Graduating from DU.

Graduating from my old, false self.

Graduating into the most empowered and authentic iteration of me.

I was progressing, leveling up, moving forward, and starting new all at the same time. And perhaps even more importantly, I was exceptionally open to whatever the universe had in store for me next.

Bring it on! I thought as I walked across the stage to shake the Dean's hand and receive my diploma.

Wearing a neoprene, forest green, tartan, long-sleeved midi dress, I looked professorial, confident, and strong. And better yet, not only did I look the part, but I actually now embraced being an intelligent, confident, independent woman in my own right. I was ready to take on the world and filled to the graduation cap with *joie de vivre*. I'd made it through the ringer, braved the turbulent depths of my personal hell, and emerged stronger for it. Like steel forged in a fiery blaze or a diamond born of pressure, I sparkled. I felt like I could tackle anything, and I was so dang ready to celebrate!

I convinced my loving family to accompany me to my favorite local steakhouse, and as we settled into a cozy booth in the back, I snuck away to the bar to squeeze The Matchmaker. I mean, of course we went to Urban Farmer, y'all.

She told me how proud she was of me, and we may have even cried a few happy tears together, maybe. *Wink.* She knew what this moment represented for me, for she had been with me through the trials and tribulations of the year and a half prior. She saw the demise of my wedding and she recognized the effort it took for me to claw my way back to this joyful and peaceful place in my life. When she said she was proud, she wasn't just talking about my graduation. She saw the woman I had become, and she knew the pain I went through to find her. *That* was what my dear friend was proud of when she squeezed me close for a love-filled hug. I squeezed her back, and unable to find the words, simply said, "I love you, friend."

She didn't need more; she knew.

"Come have a glass of wine with me at the bar after dinner so we can celebrate you properly," she said with a cheeky grin.

"You don't have to ask me twice!" I assured her, both of us now laughing and wiping our eyes simultaneously.

Back at dinner, it struck me that I was finally at complete ease with myself in an all-encompassing, self-love filled manner I hadn't experienced for years. I was secure in my life, secure in myself, and surrounded by the joy and comfort of my family and friends. What more could a girl want!? I was floating away on cloud nine and simply couldn't believe my good fortune. I was well and truly blessed.

What a difference a year makes, I thought as my phone vibrated in my lap.

Though I would normally *never* look at my phone during dinner (the horror), something told me to brave the rudeness and pick it up to take a quick peek. It was a text from The Matchmaker.

"So, I swear I did not do this…but guess who just walked in the bar?"

The gulp to end all gulps.

Almost three months after the cosmic ball first got rolling, it seemed our timing was finally right. I was going to meet Mr. Potentially Perfect after all.

Needless to say, I couldn't focus much on the rest of dinner and instead kept sneaking glances at the bar. I saw a sliver of a very handsome profile, with classic features reminiscent of a golden Roman coin. His jaw was strong, with the whisper of a five-o'-clock shadow just settling in, and he had the littlest scar on his cheek that dimpled when he smiled. His nose was angular and perfectly proportioned

KATHERINE ROSE WOLLER

atop his beautifully full lips so the overall effect of his profile had an air of regality. He was the imperfect beauty of ancient rulers personified, and the effect was striking.

I craned my neck to see more but was rudely thwarted by another patron's less handsome, less kingly potato head blocking my view. *Phooey.*

For the next hour, I was acutely aware he was there, just a mere twenty or so feet away, and I willed the dessert course to end already! No offense to my family, but mercilessly, dinner ultimately ended and I was free. I hugged my loved ones goodbye and as they headed for the door, I silently peeled off.

I made a beeline for the serendipitously open seat next to Mr. Potentially Perfect, recognizing the Tom Hardy look-alike meets Indiana Jones meets James Bond instantly from the photos The Matchmaker had shown me three months prior, and plopped my tartan-clad booty down with a thud.

He quickly turned my way, no doubt surprised by the abruptness of my arrival.

"Hi, I'm Katherine. You must be Mr. Potentially Perfect," I said as I extended my hand toward him.

"Nice to finally meet you," he replied, as a genuine, loving, beautiful smile spread across his handsome, full lips.

Cue the harps and baby cupids and swans and rose petals! Cue the lightning strikes, the moment of creation, the big bang, the illumination, the life. Cue it all. That was it. I was smitten.

Though I love music, I am not one who ever remembers who the artist is, or the name of the song even, but there is indeed a song called "Home" by Edward Sharpe and the

Magnetic Zeros that perfectly captures the reality of our meeting.

You know the song. It's a classic indie folk duet you hear in movies, when the boy and girl finally get together. The lead vocals sing out clearly, speaking of alleyways and waterfalls and the almost indescribable feeling when your heart auspiciously finds its home in the soul-soothing embrace of another. There's even a melodic whistling interlude for heartwarming good measure. That song.

Well, the lyrics go a little something like this...

Oh, home, let me come home
Home is wherever I'm with you

Like the movies, the ever-catchy chorus swam through my mind as my heart fell deeper and deeper in love with the feeling of home that resulted from being right there next to Mr. Potentially Perfect.

We were in a bar filled to the gills with other revelers, but we might as well have been alone for we were focused solely on each other. We laughed, we bantered. We over-shared. I told him about calling off my wedding, told him about this book. We closed it down. We wandered to the late-night taproom down the street.

Moats and boats and waterfalls
Alleyways and payphone calls
I've been everywhere (hey) with you

We devoured the best chicken tenders in all of Denver, effortlessly chatting all the while.

That's true, laugh until we think we'll die
Barefoot on a summer night
Never could be sweeter than with you (hey)

There's no other way to say it, but we clicked. We were like two parts of one magical whole and it was clear from night one there was no way either one of us was letting go.

Man, oh man, you're my best friend
I scream it to the nothingness
There ain't nothing that I need

We were together.
We were "Home."
It seems the Matchmaker was right all along...
Here he was, my Mr. Potentially Perfect.
The reason I had been to hell and back.
The next chapter of my life and the source of my happiness yet to come.
My future.
My Love.
My Mr. Forever.

Oh, home, yes, I am home
Home is when I'm alone with you

And by some glorious miracle, this was the start of my *true* picture-perfect wedding story.
Though that's a fairytale for another day.

Acknowledgments

Thank you to those who loved me then, to those who love me now, and to those who I will always love, endlessly and without fail.

Thank you to my husband, Joe–you are my greatest adventure and my safe space all rolled into one. You've shown me what unconditional love truly looks like and I am forever grateful we chose each other. You've supported me without question through this process as you told me time and time again to keep writing. You believed what I had to say mattered, and your encouragement made all the difference in the world. In the words of *Pride and Prejudice*'s Mr. Darcy himself, "You have bewitched me, body and soul, and I love, I love, I love you."

Thank you to my Mom, who went through hell as well, my Papa, who believed in me regardless, my sisters, whom I love and adore, my stepfather, who had my back, my aunt and uncle, who never wavered in their support, my cousins, my family, and my friends.

Thank you to those of you who also played a pivotal role in my imperfect journey of self; large or small, you were invaluable.

Thank you to Mr. Ex, The Ride or Die, The Wild One, The Single Lady, The Matchmaker, The Blonde One, The

Trusty Therapist, Mr. New Orleans, Mr. Super Star, and Mr. Tech Mega Millions.

Thank you to each and every one of you for your grace, love, anger, criticism, support, honesty and guidance. Thank you for all of it. I simply would not be here without you. For even you, my harshest critics, helped me realize what I needed to do to build a better version of self.

Thank you to those of you who specifically supported me in the journey of writing this book. Thank you to my coach, publisher, and all around book doula, Samantha; you helped bring this book to life and guided me on my path to becoming an author. To my professional editors, Megan and John. You pushed me to take this book to a new level, and even though it was a confronting process, you lovingly held my hand the whole way through. To my brilliant friend (you know who you are) who agreed to read this book in its most rudimentary form–your feedback undeniably changed the book for the better. Thank you to my interior designer, Kathryn, my cover designer, Rich, my photographer, Angelli, my web developer, Ashley, and my professional support team as a whole.

Finally, thank you to those of you who bought this book. You are the reason I wrote it in the first place. I hope it helped!

If you are interested in learning more about Katherine Rose Woller or signing up for email alerts about exciting things to come, please visit:

www.KatherineRoseWoller.com
Follow @KatherineWoller on Instagram

About the Author

As a lifelong learner and endlessly curious individual, Katherine Rose Woller has lived many lives. From art gallerina to teacher to ski industry professional to marketing executive and now author, Katherine has forever remained focused on the unifying power of storytelling. She fervently believes in the liberating impact and life affirming power that sharing one's experiences can have and embraces both the chaos and peace of what that means in practice.

Katherine is a peripatetic wanderer at heart, traveling the globe with her family as they seek to fill each moment with beautiful adventures–laughing, growing, and evolving on a daily basis. She is a passionate athlete, dedicating time to running, yoga, and skiing in her joyful pursuit of mental, physical, and spiritual wellness. In every sense, she is a woman on the move.

Bibliography

Ballard, Camisha. "Calling off your wedding: Everything you need to know." Eventsured. March 15, 2023.

Bird, Brad, director. *The Incredibles*. Pixar Animation Studios; Walt Disney Pictures, 2004,1 hr., 55 min.

Buck, Joan Juliet. "Gisele Bündchen: Earth Mother." *Vogue*, March 14, 2010.

Caldwell, Ian and Dustin Thomason, *The Rule of Four*. New York: The Dial Press, 2004, 196.

Chelsom, Peter, director. *Serendipity*. Tapestry Films; Miramax Films, 2001.

Coolidge, Martha, director. *The Prince and Me*. Lions Gate Films; Sobini Films; Epsilon Motion Pictures; Paramount Pictures; Stillking Films, 2004.

Curtis, Richard, director. *Love Actually*. Universal Pictures; StudioCanal; Working Title Films; DNA Films, 2003.

Doyle, Glennon. *Untamed*. New York: The Dial Press, 2020, 67, 73.

Edward Sharpe and the Magnetic Zeros. "Home." Recorded 2010. Track 6 on *Up From Below*. Vagrant; Rough Trade.

Gilbert, Elizabeth, *Big Magic: Creative Living Beyond Fear*. New York: Riverhead Books, 2015, 33.

Gilbert, Elizabeth, *Committed: A Love Story*. New York: Riverhead Books, 2011.

Goodreads. "Benjamin Spock > Quotes > Quotable Quote." www.goodreads.com/quotes/4422-trust-yourself-you-know-more-than-you-think-you-do.

Goodreads. "Diana, Princess of Wales > Quotes > Quotable Quote." www.goodreads.com/quotes/484811-only-do-what-your-heart-tells-you.

Goodreads. "George Addair > Quotes > Quotable Quote." https://www.goodreads.com/quotes/1216350-everything-you-ve-ever-wanted-is-on-the-other-side-of.

Goodreads. "H.G. Wells > Quotes > Quotable Quote." www.goodreads.com/quotes/140786-sometimes-you-have-to-step-outside-of-the-person-you-ve.

Goodreads. "Hunter S. Thompson > Quotes > Quotable Quote." www.goodreads.com/quotes/7429050-who-is-the-happier-man-he-who-has-braved-the.

Goodreads. "John Muir > Quotes > Quotable Quote." www.goodreads.com/quotes/7796963-and-into-the-forest-i-go-to-lose-my-mind.

Goodreads. "Oprah Winfrey > Quotes > Quotable Quote." www.goodreads.com/quotes/115063-follow-your-instincts-that-s-where-true-wisdom-manifests-itself.

Hawthorne, Nathaniel. *The Scarlet Letter*. Boston: James R. Osgood and Company, 1878.

Hemingway, Ernest. *A Farewell to Arms*. New York: Scribner, 1957, 249.

Jamie Foxx. "Blame It." Recorded 2008. Track 5 on *Intuition*. J Records.

Kennedy, Kate. *One in a millennial: On friendship, feelings, fangirls, and fitting in*. Read by author. New York, NY: Macmillan Audio, 2024.

Leder, Mimi, director. *On the Basis of Sex*. Alibaba Pictures Group; Dreamwork Pictures; Participant Media; Robert Cort Productions.

Lizzo. "About Damn Time." *Special*. Nice Life Recording; Atlantic Records. 2002.

Loehnen, Elise, host. "On Being Basic (Kate Kennedy)." *Pulling the Thread* (podcast). February 15, 2024.

Loehnen, Elise, host. "The Complexity of Weight Loss Drugs (Johann Hari)." *Pulling the Thread* (podcast). May 9, 2024.

Luke Bryan. "Sunrise, Sunburn, Sunset." *What Makes You Country*. Capitol Records Nashville. 2017.

Maria Popova. "The Stoic's Key to Peace of Mind: Seneca on the Antidote to Anxiety." *The Marginalian*. August 27, 2017.

Murphy, Ryan, director. *Eat, Pray, Love*. Columbia Pictures; Plan B Entertainment. 2010.

National Diamond Syndicate Inc. "Engagement season? 2023-24 should see strong rebound in marriage proposals."

Phantom Planet. "California." *The Guest*. Epic Records. 2001.

Rodgers, Richard (music) & Hammerstein, Oscar II (lyrics). "So Long, Farewell." *The Sound of Music*. Rodgers & Hammerstein Organization. 1959, 1960.

Simpson, Jessica. *Open Book: A Memoir*. Read by author. New York: HarperAudio, 2020.

Stoller, Nicholas, director. *Forgetting Sarah Marshall*. Apatow Productions; Universal Pictures, 2008.

Tennant, Andy, director. *Ever After: A Cinderella Story*. Twentieth Century Fox, 1998.

The Darkness. "I Believe in a Thing Called Love." *Permission to Land*. Atlantic Records. 2002.

Wiest, Brianna. *The Pivot Year: 365 Days to Become the Person You Truly Want To Be.* Brooklyn: Thought Catalog Books, 2023, Day 152.

Wilde, Oscar. *An Ideal Husband.* London: Methuen & Company, 1914.

William Ernest Henley. "Invictus." *A Book of Verses.* London: D. Nutt, 1888.

Winfrey, Oprah. "What Oprah Knows for Sure About Life's Biggest Adventure." *O, The Oprah Magazine.* July, 2002.

Wright, Joe, director. *Pride and Prejudice.* Universal Pictures; StudioCanal; Working Title Films; Scion Films, 2005.

Yakin, Boaz, director. *Uptown Girls.* Metro-Goldwyn-Mayer; GreeneStreet Films, 2003.